MAKING MONEY ON YOUTUBE WITHOUT MAKING VIDEOS

By Alexander J. Kelley

Making Money on YouTube Without Making Videos

Copyright © 2023 by Alexander J. Kelley

Book Cover by Alexander J. Kelley

First Edition 2003

www.alexanderkelley.com

To my son, Greyson.
From the moment you were born, everything in this world seemed possible. I love you, papi.

Table of Contents

Introduction

Introduction

What to Expect from this Book

Welcome to "Making Money on YouTube Without Making Videos!" This book is your ultimate guide to understanding how you can monetize YouTube without ever creating your own videos. Whether you're a content creator looking for alternative ways to earn money on YouTube, or simply someone interested in exploring creative ways to generate income online, this book is for you.

Inside, you'll discover a step-by-step approach to leveraging YouTube's massive audience and earning potential without the need to produce original videos. We'll delve into the various strategies and techniques that can turn your YouTube channel into a money-making machine. From affiliate marketing and sponsorships to unique and out-of-the-box ideas, this book will provide you with practical tips, resources, and insights to help you achieve your financial goals.

You'll learn how to navigate YouTube's monetization policies, set up your own YouTube channel for maximum earning potential, optimize your content for monetization, and leverage various income streams to generate revenue. We'll also explore 20 unique and creative ways to make money on YouTube without creating videos, discussing the potential benefits, challenges, and tips for getting started with each method.

Whether you're a seasoned YouTuber looking to diversify your income streams, an aspiring content creator looking for alternative ways to earn money on YouTube, or simply someone interested in the fascinating world of YouTube monetization, this book will provide you with the knowledge and tools to unlock the full potential of YouTube as a money-making platform.

Get ready to unlock the secrets of making money on YouTube without making videos and embark on an exciting journey to financial success. Let's turn your YouTube channel into a money machine!

Chapter 1: Introduction to the YouTube Money Making Machine

Chapter 1

The Growing Popularity of YouTube

YouTube has rapidly become one of the most popular platforms for content creation and sharing, attracting billions of viewers from around the world. With its vast user base, diverse content offerings, and robust monetization opportunities, YouTube has emerged as a lucrative platform for individuals, businesses, and marketers to make money online. In this chapter, we will explore the incredible growth and popularity of YouTube and why it presents an exciting opportunity for marketers seeking to generate passive income through social media and digital marketing.

YouTube's astronomical growth in recent years cannot be understated. With over 2 billion logged-in monthly active users and over 1 billion hours of video watched every day, YouTube has become a dominant force in the online entertainment and information landscape. It has also transformed into a platform where content creators can build dedicated audiences, engage with viewers, and monetize their content in various ways. As a marketer, understanding the scale and reach of YouTube can open new avenues for generating revenue and building a sustainable online business.

YouTube's appeal as a platform for content consumption spans across all age groups and demographics, making it a powerful tool for reaching a wide audience. From educational tutorials, product reviews, vlogs, gaming, lifestyle content, and more, YouTube caters to a diverse range of interests and niches. This diverse content ecosystem creates ample opportunities for marketers to find their niche and connect with their target audience, regardless of their industry or niche.

The increasing popularity of YouTube is further fueled by the growing trend of video consumption. Video has become the preferred medium of content consumption for many online users, with its engaging and interactive nature. YouTube, with its vast library of videos covering virtually any topic, has become the go-to platform for video content, making it an ideal platform for marketers to leverage for their business.

Moreover, YouTube's monetization policies and opportunities have evolved, providing content creators with more ways to earn money. The YouTube Partner Program (YPP) allows creators to monetize their content through ads, memberships, merchandise, and more. Additionally, YouTube has also opened avenues for sponsored content, brand partnerships, and affiliate marketing, providing additional ways for content creators to generate revenue from their videos.

The popularity of YouTube has also been fueled by the growing trend of cord-cutting and the rise of online streaming. Traditional TV viewership has declined, and more users are turning to online platforms like YouTube for their entertainment and information needs. This shift in consumer behavior presents a unique opportunity for marketers to tap into the growing popularity of YouTube and reach their target audience in a more personalized and engaging way.

As a marketer new to the world of making money with YouTube, understanding the growing popularity of the platform and its impact on the online content landscape is crucial. YouTube's immense reach, diverse content offerings, and evolving monetization opportunities make it an exciting platform for marketers to explore and leverage to generate passive income and grow their online business.

In the following chapters, we will delve deeper into the strategies and techniques for making money on YouTube without creating videos, including affiliate marketing, sponsorships, and other creative ways to monetize your channel. We will provide step-by-step instructions, tips, and best practices to help you embark on your YouTube money-making journey with confidence and excitement. So, buckle up and get ready to unlock the full potential of YouTube as a money-making machine!

Chapter 1

No Videos, No Problem

The idea of making money on YouTube without creating videos might sound unconventional, but it's a strategy that has gained traction among savvy marketers. The concept revolves around leveraging existing videos on YouTube and monetizing them through various methods. This approach allows marketers to tap into the vast library of videos on YouTube and earn money without the need for content creation, production, or editing.

One popular method of making money on YouTube without creating videos is through affiliate marketing. Affiliate marketing involves promoting products or services in videos created by other content creators and earning a commission for each sale or referral made through your affiliate links. This approach allows marketers to leverage the popularity of existing videos to drive sales and earn commissions, without the need to create their own videos.

Another approach is through sponsored content or brand partnerships. Marketers can collaborate with content creators who have a significant following on YouTube and create sponsored videos where they promote a brand, product, or service. This can be done through product reviews, testimonials, or endorsements, and can result in earning fees or commissions for the promotion.

Additionally, marketers can also explore the concept of re-purposing existing videos to create their own unique content. This can involve curating and compiling videos from different creators to create compilations, highlight reels, or themed playlists. By adding value through curation, organization, and presentation, marketers can create their own videos without the need for original content creation.

One more creative approach to making money on YouTube without creating videos is through commentary or reaction videos. Marketers can watch and react to existing videos, providing their own insights, comments, and reactions, and monetize these videos through ads or sponsorships. This approach allows marketers to leverage the popularity of existing videos while providing their own unique perspective and commentary.

The concept of making money on YouTube without creating videos opens a world of opportunities for marketers seeking to generate passive income and grow their online business. It allows for creative and innovative approaches to monetize videos, tap into existing content, and leverage the popularity of YouTube without the need for content creation from scratch.

However, it's important to note that this approach still requires ethical and legal considerations. Marketers need to ensure that they comply with YouTube's policies and guidelines, as well as disclose any sponsored content or affiliate partnerships according to relevant regulations. Transparency and authenticity are crucial in maintaining the trust and credibility of the audience.

In the following chapters, we will delve deeper into the strategies and techniques for making money on YouTube without creating videos, including in-depth guides on affiliate marketing, sponsored content, curation, and commentary videos.

We will provide step-by-step instructions, tips, and best practices to help marketers navigate this unique approach to monetizing YouTube and generate passive income. So, get ready to explore the exciting world of making money on YouTube without creating videos and unlock new possibilities for your online business!

Chapter 1

Potential Benefits of this Approach

The concept of making money on YouTube without creating videos offers a host of potential benefits for marketers looking to monetize their efforts in the digital space. In this chapter, we will explore the exciting advantages of this unique approach and how it can be a game-changer for marketers new to the world of YouTube, passive income, social media, and digital marketing.

1. Low Barrier to Entry: One of the significant benefits of making money on YouTube without creating videos is the low barrier to entry. Unlike traditional content creation that requires investing in cameras, equipment, and editing software, this approach allows marketers to start with minimal investment. By leveraging existing videos, marketers can tap into the vast library of content on YouTube without the need for expensive production equipment or technical expertise.

2. Time and Effort Saving: Creating original videos can be time-consuming and labor-intensive. However, with this approach, marketers can save significant time and effort by leveraging existing videos. By curating, repurposing, or providing commentary on existing content, marketers can generate income without spending extensive time and effort on content creation. This allows for more efficient use of resources and frees up time to focus on other aspects of their marketing strategy.

3. Diverse Monetization Opportunities: Making money on YouTube without creating videos provides marketers with

diverse monetization opportunities. From affiliate marketing and sponsored content to ads and sponsorships, marketers can explore various avenues to earn revenue. This diversity allows for flexibility in generating income and exploring multiple revenue streams, providing a higher potential for earnings.

4. Leveraging Existing Popularity: YouTube is already a massive platform with billions of users and videos. By leveraging existing popular videos, marketers can tap into the already established popularity and reach of those videos. This can lead to higher visibility, engagement, and potential sales, as marketers are leveraging the popularity of existing videos to generate income.

5. Scalability and Passive Income: Another significant benefit of this approach is the potential for scalability and passive income. Once the monetization methods are set up, marketers can continue to earn income from these videos without continuous effort, allowing for passive income streams. Additionally, this approach provides scalability as marketers can leverage multiple videos, niches, or content creators to generate income, increasing their earning potential.

6. Creativity and Innovation: Making money on YouTube without creating videos allows marketers to get creative and innovative with their approach. From curation and compilation videos to commentary and reaction videos, marketers have the freedom to experiment with different formats and ideas. This can result in unique and engaging content that stands out in a saturated digital landscape, providing a competitive edge.

7. Flexibility and Adaptability: This approach offers flexibility and adaptability, allowing marketers to pivot and adjust their strategy as needed. Since marketers are not tied to creating original videos, they can easily switch gears or try different approaches based on market trends, audience preferences, or their own business goals. This flexibility allows for agility in adapting to changing circumstances and staying relevant in the ever-evolving digital landscape.

8. Diversification of Income: Making money on YouTube without creating videos allows for diversification of income sources. By exploring multiple monetization methods, marketers can diversify their income streams and reduce dependence on a single source of revenue. This diversification can provide a more stable and resilient income model, mitigating risks associated with relying solely on one monetization method.

9. Opportunity for Collaboration: Collaborations and partnerships are prevalent in the YouTube community. By making money on YouTube without creating videos, marketers can leverage existing content creators' popularity and collaborate with them for sponsored content or affiliate marketing. This opens up opportunities for mutually beneficial partnerships, expanding the reach and potential earnings.

The concept of making money on YouTube without creating your own videos presents a unique and exciting opportunity for marketers looking to generate income through YouTube. It offers numerous potential benefits, including low barrier to entry, time and effort savings, diverse monetization opportunities, leverage of existing popularity, scalability and passive income potential, creativity and innovation, flexibility and adaptability, diversification of income, and opportunities for collaboration. By leveraging existing videos on YouTube, marketers can tap into the vast library of content, reach a wider audience, and potentially generate income passively. With the right strategy, dedication, and marketing skills, this approach can become a lucrative and sustainable source of revenue in the world of YouTube and digital marketing. So, buckle up and get ready to unlock the potential of YouTube as a money-making machine!

Chapter 2: Understanding YouTube and its Monetization Policies

Chapter 2

Overview of the YouTube Platform

Before we dive into the nitty-gritty of making money on YouTube, let's take a step back and get a bird's-eye view of the platform itself. YouTube is a behemoth in the online world, with over 2 billion monthly active users and over a billion hours of video watched every day. It's not just a place to watch cat videos and funny memes; it's a platform where businesses and individuals alike can build their brand, connect with audiences, and make money.

1. YouTube as a Social Media and Video Sharing Platform: YouTube is not just a video hosting platform, but also a social media platform that allows users to upload, share, comment, like, and engage with videos. With over 2 billion logged-in monthly active users, YouTube provides a massive audience to marketers who are looking to leverage its reach and engagement.

2. Monetization Opportunities on YouTube: One of the primary reasons why marketers are interested in YouTube is the potential to make money from their videos. YouTube offers various monetization options, such as ads, sponsorships, merchandise sales, and channel memberships, which can generate revenue for content creators.

3. Passive Income Potential: YouTube has the potential to generate passive income, which means that once you upload a video and monetize it, you can continue to earn money from it over time, even when you're not actively creating new content. This passive income potential makes

YouTube an attractive platform for marketers who are looking for ways to earn money even when they're not actively working on their videos.

4. Leverage Existing Popularity: YouTube is a platform that has many popular videos and content creators with massive followings. By leveraging existing popular videos, marketers can tap into the existing popularity and reach a wider audience. This can be beneficial for marketers who are new to YouTube and looking to gain visibility and grow their channel quickly.

5. Scalability and Flexibility: YouTube offers scalability, which means that you can start small and grow your channel over time as you gain more experience and traction. YouTube also offers flexibility in terms of content creation, allowing marketers to create a wide range of videos, from tutorials, vlogs, reviews, and more, depending on their niche and target audience.

6. Diverse Monetization Options: YouTube offers diverse monetization options, which means that marketers have the flexibility to choose the best approach that fits their content and audience. From ads, sponsorships, merchandise sales, and channel memberships, to crowdfunding, affiliate marketing, and more, YouTube provides a range of options to monetize content and generate income.

7. Creativity and Innovation: YouTube encourages creativity and innovation, allowing marketers to create unique and original content that resonates with their audience. This opens up opportunities for marketers to showcase their creativity, unique perspectives, and ideas, and build a loyal fan base.

8. Opportunities for Collaboration: YouTube offers opportunities for collaboration, allowing marketers to collaborate with other content creators and leverage each other's audience and expertise. Collaborations can help marketers expand their reach, gain exposure to new audiences, and create mutually beneficial partnerships.

9. Analytical Tools and Insights: YouTube provides powerful analytical tools and insights that can help marketers understand their audience, track their video performance, and make data-driven decisions. This allows marketers to optimize their content, engagement, and monetization strategies for better results.

10. Global Reach: YouTube has a global reach, with users from all over the world. This provides marketers with an opportunity to reach a diverse audience and expand their brand's reach beyond their local market.

YouTube offers an exciting and lucrative platform for marketers who are looking to make money with their videos. With its massive user base, diverse monetization options, passive income potential, scalability, flexibility, creativity, collaboration opportunities, and analytical tools, YouTube provides a wealth of benefits for marketers.

Chapter 2

Monetization Policies and Requirements

When it comes to making money on YouTube, understanding the platform's monetization policies and requirements is crucial. YouTube has specific guidelines in place to ensure that creators are producing high-quality content and adhering to community guidelines.

To be eligible for monetization on YouTube, you need to meet certain requirements. One of the key requirements is the YouTube Partner Program (YPP), which allows creators to monetize their content through ads, sponsorships, and other means. To join the YPP, you need to have at least 1,000 subscribers and 4,000 watch hours in the past 12 months. We will discuss in detail how to meet these requirements and strategies to grow your channel to meet them.

Beyond the subscriber and watch hours requirements, YouTube also has strict policies in place regarding the content that is eligible for monetization. Creators need to comply with community guidelines, which include rules on copyright, violence, nudity, hate speech, and other sensitive topics. We will go through these guidelines in detail, providing practical tips on how to create content that aligns with YouTube's policies and maximizes your chances of monetization.

In addition to the general monetization policies, YouTube also has specific policies for ad placement, product integrations, and sponsored content. Understanding these policies is crucial to avoid violations that could result in demonetization or other penalties. We will discuss the various types of ads on YouTube, including pre-roll ads, mid-roll ads, and overlay ads, and how to optimize ad placements for maximum revenue.

YouTube also has policies regarding paid product integrations, endorsements, and sponsored content. We will cover the disclosure requirements for sponsored content, including the use of disclaimers, product placements, and affiliate marketing. We will also discuss strategies for finding sponsored opportunities, negotiating deals, and building long-term partnerships with brands.

Lastly, we will explore alternative monetization methods beyond the YouTube Partner Program. These may include crowdfunding, merchandise sales, fan subscriptions, and other creative ways to generate revenue from your YouTube channel. We will provide practical tips and examples of successful monetization strategies to inspire you to think outside the box and diversify your income streams.

Understanding the monetization policies and requirements of YouTube is essential for anyone looking to make money on the platform. It ensures that you comply with YouTube's guidelines, avoid violations, and maximize your revenue potential.

Chapter 2

Creating Content Without Making Videos

As a marketer looking to leverage the YouTube platform for income, you might think that creating videos is the only way to generate content. However, the good news is that YouTube offers various avenues for content creation beyond traditional videos. In this chapter, we'll explore alternative methods of creating engaging content on YouTube without making videos, and how you can utilize them to build your online presence and monetize your channel.

1. Animated Videos: You can create animated videos using animation software or online tools, such as Powtoon or Vyond. Animated videos can be used to convey information, tell stories, or present ideas in a visually engaging and creative way.

2. ASMR Audio: You can create ASMR (Autonomous Sensory Meridian Response) audio content, which focuses on relaxing sounds, whispers, or soft voices that create a calming and soothing experience for viewers. ASMR audio can be uploaded to YouTube as a standalone video or combined with visuals, such as images or text overlays.

3. Audio Blogs or Vlogs: You can create audio blogs or vlogs, where you record your thoughts, opinions, or stories as an audio file and upload it to YouTube. You can use static images, text overlays, or other visual elements to accompany the audio and create a compelling video.

4. Compilation Videos: You can create compilation videos by curating and compiling existing videos from other creators or sources. This can include compilations of

funny moments, best-ofs, top 10 lists, or other types of content.

5. Guided Meditation: You can create guided meditation videos that provide relaxation, stress relief, and mindfulness exercises for viewers. You can use calming visuals, soothing music, and your own voice to guide viewers through meditation sessions that focus on deep breathing, body awareness, and mental relaxation. Guided meditation videos can be a valuable resource for those looking to improve their mental well-being, reduce stress, and cultivate mindfulness in their daily lives.

6. Hiring a Freelancer: If you're looking to create high-quality content for your YouTube channel but lack the time, skills, or resources to do so, you can hire a freelancer to create custom-made content for you. This can include hiring a voiceover artist to provide narration, a graphic designer to create visuals, or a video editor to polish your videos. Collaborating with freelancers can help you bring your creative vision to life and elevate the overall quality of your YouTube content.

7. Live Streams: You can create live streams on YouTube without creating pre-recorded videos. Live streams can include Q&A sessions, discussions, tutorials, or other interactive content that engages viewers in real-time.

8. Podcasts: You can create audio-only content, such as podcasts, and upload them to YouTube. You can use platforms like Anchor, SoundCloud, or other podcast hosting services to create and distribute your podcast episodes on YouTube.

9. Record Your Own Music: If you're musically inclined, you can create your own music and upload it to YouTube.

Whether you're a singer, songwriter, or instrumentalist, you can use music recording software, instruments, or vocals to create original songs, covers, or instrumental tracks. You can also collaborate with other musicians to create unique music for your YouTube channel and share your talent and passion with your audience. Creating your own music can add a personal touch to your videos and help you showcase your creativity and musical abilities.

10. Screen Recordings: You can create videos by recording your screen while performing tasks or demonstrating processes on your computer. This can include tutorials, software reviews, or presentations that showcase your expertise in a particular area.

11. Slideshow or Image-Based Videos: You can create videos by compiling images, photos, or slideshows and adding background music or voiceovers. You can use software or online tools to create visually appealing videos with images and music to share on YouTube.

12. Sound Effects Videos: You can create videos that feature various sound effects, such as nature sounds, city noises, or other ambient sounds. These videos can be used for relaxation, meditation, or to enhance other types of content, such as tutorials, presentations, or storytelling videos.

13. Stock and Royalty-Free Videos: You can create videos using stock footage or royalty-free videos that are available online. These videos can be used to create visually appealing content without the need for original video footage. You can find stock footage or royalty-free videos from websites or platforms that offer free or paid options for content creators to use in their videos.

14. Text-Based Videos: You can create videos using text-based content, such as quotes, poems, stories, or other written content, with appropriate visuals and background music. This can be a creative way to share written content on YouTube in a visually appealing format.

15. Whiteboard Videos: You can create whiteboard videos using software or online tools that simulate the process of drawing on a whiteboard while explaining concepts or ideas. Whiteboard videos can be a unique and engaging way to present information and engage viewers. Free plans can be found with RawShorts (www.rawshorts.com), Powtoon (www.powtoon.com), and Moovly (www.moovly.com).

16. Repurposing Content: If you have created content in other formats, such as blogs, podcasts, or ebooks, you can repurpose that content into YouTube videos and monetize it. For example, if you have written a blog post on a particular topic, you can convert it into a script and create a video around that topic. You can also turn your podcast episodes into videos by adding visual elements or creating video highlights. Repurposing content can save you time and effort while still allowing you to monetize your knowledge and expertise on YouTube.

Unlocking the potential of content creation without relying on videos is entirely possible with the abundance of free tools and resources available. For marketers venturing into the realm of YouTube as a revenue stream, there is a wealth of options to explore. Here, we've compiled a comprehensive list of these resources, providing an invaluable guide for those looking to create content without having to produce videos:

1. Canva (www.canva.com): Canva offers a user-friendly platform with pre-designed templates for creating text overlays, captions, subtitles, and other graphic elements that can be added to your videos. It has a wide range of fonts, colors, and customization options to match your branding and create visually appealing text-based content.

2. Google Docs (docs.google.com): Google Docs is a free online document editing tool that can be used to create transcripts, scripts, or captions for your videos. It offers collaboration features, allowing you to work with team members or editors in real-time, and convert your text-based content into different formats for easy sharing or distribution.

3. YouTube Captioning (www.youtube.com): YouTube itself provides a built-in captioning feature that allows you to add captions or subtitles to your videos. This not only makes your content more accessible but also improves searchability and discoverability on YouTube.

4. Pixlr (pixlr.com): Pixlr is a free online photo editing tool that can be used to create custom text overlays or graphics for your videos. It offers a wide range of design features, including text editing, filters, and effects, to enhance your text-based content.

5. Subtitle Edit (www.nikse.dk/SubtitleEdit): Subtitle Edit is a free software for creating and editing subtitles for videos. It allows you to create subtitles in multiple languages, customize fonts, colors, and timings, and export subtitles in different formats.

6. Unsplash (unsplash.com): Unsplash is a website that offers free stock images that can be used in your text-based

content. It has a wide collection of high-quality images that can enhance the visual appeal of your content.

7. Pixabay (pixabay.com): Pixabay is another website that offers free stock images, as well as videos and illustrations, that can be used in your text-based content. It has a vast collection of visual assets that can add visual interest to your content.

8. Google Fonts (fonts.google.com): Google Fonts is a website that offers a wide selection of free fonts that can be used in your text-based content. You can search for fonts based on different styles, languages, or popularity, and easily download them for use in your content.

9. Pexels (www.pexels.com): Pexels is a website that offers free stock photos, videos, and music that can be used in your text-based content. It has a large collection of high-quality visual assets that can add depth and creativity to your content.

10. Flaticon (www.flaticon.com): Flaticon is a website that offers free icons and vector graphics that can be used in your text-based content. It has a vast library of icons in different styles and formats that can enhance the visual appeal of your content.

11. Google Drive (drive.google.com): Google Drive is a free cloud storage and file-sharing platform that can be used to store and share your text-based content with team members, editors, or collaborators. It offers a wide range of file formats, including documents, presentations, and spreadsheets, that can be used for content creation.

12. Grammarly (www.grammarly.com): Grammarly is a free online writing tool that can be used to check and correct grammar, spelling, and punctuation errors in your text-

based content. It helps you create professional-looking content with proper grammar and writing style.

13. Trello (trello.com): Trello is a free project management tool that can be used to organize and manage your content creation process. You can create boards, lists, and cards to keep track of your ideas, tasks, and deadlines, making it easy to collaborate with team members or manage your content creation workflow.

14. Social Media Scheduling Tools: There are several free social media scheduling tools available, such as Hootsuite (www.hootsuite.com), Buffer (buffer.com), and Later (later.com), that allow you to schedule and automate your text-based content across different social media platforms. These tools can help you streamline your content distribution process and save time.

15. SoundCloud (soundcloud.com): SoundCloud is a free audio hosting platform that can be used to create and share audio content, such as podcasts or audio clips. You can record, upload, and edit audio content using their online tools, and embed the content in your text-based content for added engagement.

16. Infogram (infogram.com): Infogram is a free infographic creation tool that allows you to create visually appealing infographics to convey complex information in a visual format. You can customize the templates, charts, and graphics to create engaging infographics for your text-based content.

17. SlideShare (www.slideshare.net): SlideShare is a free platform for creating and sharing presentations, documents, and slideshows. You can create visual presentations with text-based content and share them on

social media or embed them in your website or blog to enhance your content.

18. Google Trends (trends.google.com): Google Trends is a free tool that allows you to discover popular search queries and topics. You can use it to identify trending topics and keywords related to your content, and create text-based content around those topics to drive traffic and engagement.

19. AnswerThePublic (answerthepublic.com): AnswerThePublic is a free tool that generates content ideas based on popular questions people are asking on search engines. You can use it to discover common questions related to your niche or industry and create text-based content that provides answers to those questions.

YouTube offers various avenues for content creation beyond traditional videos. By utilizing free tools and resources such as graphic design tools, text editing tools, stock images, and social media scheduling tools, you can create engaging and visually appealing content for your audience. With creativity and strategic use of these resources, you can generate compelling text-based content that resonates with your audience and drives traffic to your YouTube channel or other digital marketing efforts.

Don't limit yourself to videos alone but explore the multitude of options available to create unique and captivating content that helps you build your online presence and monetize your channel. YouTube is a powerful platform with diverse content creation opportunities, so embrace the possibilities and unlock new avenues for success.

Chapter 3: Creating a YouTube Channel & Optimizing for Monetization

Chapter 3

Step-by-Step Instructions for Creating a YouTube Channel

Welcome to the exciting world of YouTube! In this chapter, we will walk you through the step-by-step process of creating your own YouTube channel. Whether you're a marketer new to the world of making money with YouTube, seeking passive income, or looking to expand your digital marketing efforts, creating a YouTube channel can be a valuable tool to connect with your target audience, share your content, and monetize your channel.

Step 1: Sign up for a Google Account

To create a YouTube channel, you'll need a Google Account. If you already have one, you can skip this step. If you don't have a Google Account, you can easily create one by going to the Google Account creation page (https://accounts.google.com/signup) and following the prompts to set up your account. Make sure to choose an email address that is professional and associated with your brand or content.

Step 2: Go to YouTube.com and Sign in

Once you have a Google Account, go to YouTube.com and sign in using your Google Account credentials. If you're already signed into your Google Account, you'll automatically be signed in to YouTube as well.

Step 3: Click on the Profile Icon and Select "Create a Channel"

In the top-right corner of the YouTube homepage, you'll see a profile icon. Click on it, and a drop-down menu will appear. Select the "Create a Channel" option from the menu.

Step 4: Choose a Channel Name and Category

Next, you'll need to choose a name for your YouTube channel. This is an important decision as it will be the identity of your channel and how viewers will recognize your content. Choose a name that is memorable, reflects your brand or content, and is aligned with your target audience.

You'll also need to select a category for your channel. This category will help YouTube understand the type of content you plan to create, and it will assist viewers in discovering your content. Choose a category that accurately represents the main focus of your channel.

Step 5: Customize Your Channel

Once you've chosen a channel name and category, you'll have the option to customize your channel. You can upload a profile picture and channel art that reflects your brand or content. Use high-quality images that are visually appealing and represent your channel's personality. You can also add a channel description that provides a brief overview of your content and what viewers can expect from your channel.

Step 6: Upload Your First Video

Now that your channel is set up, it's time to start uploading your content. Click on the "Upload" button in the top-right corner of your YouTube homepage and select "Upload video" from the drop-down menu. Choose the video file from your computer, add a title, description, and relevant tags to help viewers find your content. You can also choose a thumbnail image for your video that is engaging and captures viewers' attention.

Step 7: Optimize Your Video

To make your video more discoverable, it's essential to optimize it. Add relevant keywords in your video title, description, and tags that are aligned with your content and target audience. Use a compelling and informative video description that provides context about your content and encourages viewers to watch. You can also add annotations, end screens, and cards to promote other videos, playlists, or external websites.

Step 8: Promote Your Channel

Creating a YouTube channel is just the beginning. To grow your channel and attract viewers, you'll need to promote it. Share your videos on social media platforms, embed them on your website or blog, and collaborate with other YouTubers or influencers in your niche. Engage with your viewers through comments, respond to their feedback, and encourage them to subscribe to your channel. Utilize SEO techniques, such as optimizing your video titles, descriptions, and tags with relevant keywords, to improve your channel's visibility in search results. Consider running paid promotions or advertising campaigns to reach a wider audience and gain more subscribers.

Step 9: Create Consistent and Engaging Content

Consistency is key to building a successful YouTube channel. Plan a content schedule and stick to it, whether it's weekly, bi-weekly, or monthly. Create engaging and high-quality content that resonates with your target audience and provides value. Consider different types of content, such as tutorials, reviews, vlogs, interviews, or behind-the-scenes footage, to keep your content fresh and interesting. Remember to always prioritize your viewers' needs and interests and encourage them to like, comment, and share your videos.

Step 10: Build a Community

Building a community around your YouTube channel is crucial for long-term success. Respond to comments, engage with your viewers on social media, and create a sense of community by encouraging discussions and feedback. Encourage viewers to subscribe to your channel and turn on notifications to stay updated with your latest content. Consider hosting live streams, Q&A sessions, or collaborations with other creators to further connect with your audience and foster a loyal community.

Step 11: Monetize Your Channel

Once your channel has gained traction and has a substantial following, you can start monetizing it. YouTube offers several ways to make money from your channel, such as through Google AdSense, sponsored content, merchandise sales, and crowdfunding. Familiarize yourself with YouTube's Partner Program and its guidelines for monetization, and follow the necessary steps to enable monetization on your channel. Keep in mind that building a successful and monetizable channel takes time, effort, and consistency.

Step 12: Analyze and Optimize Your Performance

Regularly analyze your channel's performance and make data-driven decisions to optimize your content and grow your channel. Utilize YouTube's analytics tools to gain insights into your viewership, engagement, demographics, and traffic sources. Identify your most successful videos and content types and replicate their success. Experiment with different strategies, such as changing your video titles, descriptions, thumbnails, or posting schedule, to see what resonates best with your audience. Continuously iterate and improve your content to keep your channel relevant and engaging.

Step 13: Stay Current with YouTube's Policies and Best Practices

YouTube's policies and best practices are subject to change, so it's crucial to stay informed and compliant. Familiarize yourself with YouTube's Community Guidelines, copyright policies, and terms of service, and ensure that your content adheres to these guidelines. Stay updated with YouTube's latest features, tools, and algorithm changes, and adapt your content and strategies accordingly. Engage with YouTube's Creator Academy, forums, and community for valuable insights, tips, and support from fellow creators.

Step 14: Stay Engaged with Your Audience and Adapt Your Content

As your channel grows, it's important to stay engaged with your audience and adapt your content to their changing needs and interests. Listen to your viewers' feedback, comments, and suggestions, and incorporate them into your content strategy. Keep an open dialogue with your audience and build a genuine connection with them. Respond to comments, messages, and inquiries in a timely and professional manner, and show appreciation for their support. Continuously strive to improve your content and provide value to your audience to maintain their loyalty and engagement.

Step 15: Keep Learning and Experimenting

The world of YouTube is constantly evolving, so it's crucial to keep learning, experimenting, and staying updated with the latest trends and best practices. Stay curious, be open to trying new things, and learn from your successes and failures. Keep honing your skills in video creation, editing, and marketing. Stay updated with the latest advancements in YouTube's features, algorithms, and policies. Attend industry events, workshops, and webinars to learn from experienced creators and industry experts. Experiment with different content formats, video lengths, and styles to see what resonates best with your audience. Don't be afraid to take risks and try new ideas to keep your channel fresh and exciting.

Creating a successful YouTube channel requires careful planning, consistent effort, and a deep understanding of your target audience. By following these step-by-step instructions, you can lay a solid foundation for your YouTube channel and increase your chances of success in the world of digital marketing and passive income.

Remember to prioritize creating high-quality content that resonates with your audience, engage with your viewers & build a community, optimize your channel's performance, stay updated with YouTube's policies & best practices, and continuously learn and experiment to stay ahead of the curve. With dedication, creativity, and persistence, you can build a thriving YouTube channel that generates revenue and helps you achieve your marketing and financial goals.

Chapter 3

Setting Up a Channel for Monetization

If you're a marketer looking to make money with YouTube, setting up your channel for monetization is a crucial step. YouTube offers several options for creators to earn revenue from their content, including ads, merchandise sales, channel memberships, and more. Here is the step-by-step process of setting up a YouTube channel for monetization, from creating an account to meeting the eligibility requirements and optimizing your channel for maximum earning potential.

Step 1: Create a YouTube Account

To start monetizing your content on YouTube, you'll need to create a YouTube account if you don't have one already. Go to youtube.com and click on the "Sign In" button in the top right corner. You can sign in with your existing Google account or create a new one specifically for your YouTube channel. Choose a unique and memorable username that reflects your brand or content niche.

Step 2: Customize Your Channel

Once you've created your YouTube account, it's time to customize your channel to make it visually appealing and engaging for your audience. Upload a profile picture that represents your brand or content and create a channel art/banner that reflects your channel's theme or message. Write an engaging channel description that gives an overview of what your channel is about and what viewers can expect from your content. You can also add links to your website, social media accounts, and other relevant resources.

Step 3: Create High-Quality Content

To monetize your YouTube channel, you need to create high-quality content that adheres to YouTube's community guidelines and copyright policies. Invest in good-quality equipment, such as a camera, microphone, and lighting, to ensure that your videos have professional production value. Plan your content carefully, keeping in mind your target audience and the goals of your channel. Create engaging, informative, and entertaining videos that resonate with your viewers and keep them coming back for more.

Step 4: Meet the Monetization Eligibility Requirements

YouTube has certain eligibility requirements that creators need to meet before they can start monetizing their content. As of the time of writing this book, the requirements include:

1. Having at least 4,000 hours of watch time in the last 12 months
2. Having at least 1,000 subscribers
3. Adhering to YouTube's community guidelines and copyright policies

Meeting these requirements may take time and effort, but it's essential to build a solid foundation for monetizing your channel.

Step 5: Apply for the YouTube Partner Program (YPP)

Once you've met the eligibility requirements, you can apply for the YouTube Partner Program (YPP), which allows you to monetize your content through ads, merchandise sales, and other revenue streams. To apply for YPP, go to youtube.com/monetization and follow the on-screen instructions to submit your application. YouTube will review your channel to ensure that it complies with their policies and guidelines, and if approved, you'll receive an email notification confirming that you're now part of the YPP.

Step 6: Optimize Your Videos for Ads

To maximize your earning potential from ads, it's essential to optimize your videos for ads. You can choose different ad formats, such as pre-roll ads, mid-roll ads, or end-screen ads, and strategically place them in your videos to minimize disruption to your viewers' experience. Experiment with different ad placements and monitor their performance to find what works best for your content and audience. Remember to always adhere to YouTube's ad policies and guidelines to avoid any issues with monetization.

Step 7: Explore Other Monetization Options

In addition to ads, YouTube offers other monetization options that you can explore to diversify your revenue streams. These options include merchandise sales, channel memberships, and donations from your viewers. You can set up an online store to sell branded merchandise, such as t-shirts, mugs, or other items related to your content or brand. You can also offer channel memberships, which allow your viewers to access exclusive content, perks, or community features in exchange for a monthly fee. Another option is to enable the "Super Chat" feature, which allows viewers to make donations during live streams or premieres. Exploring these additional monetization options can help you maximize your earning potential on YouTube.

Step 8: Engage with Your Audience

Building a loyal and engaged audience is essential for monetizing your YouTube channel. Respond to comments on your videos, engage with your viewers on social media, and create a sense of community around your channel. Ask for feedback, listen to your viewers' suggestions, and incorporate their input into your content. By nurturing a strong relationship with your audience, you can increase their loyalty and support, which can translate into higher engagement, more views, and ultimately more revenue.

Step 9: Continuously Improve Your Content

To stay competitive on YouTube and attract more viewers and revenue, it's crucial to continuously improve your content. Pay attention to your video metrics, such as watch time, engagement rate, and audience retention, to gain insights into what resonates with your audience and what can be improved. Experiment with different content formats, styles, and topics to keep your content fresh and interesting. Stay updated with the latest trends and best practices in digital marketing, social media, and YouTube, and be willing to adapt and evolve your content strategy accordingly.

Step 10: Promote Your Channel

To increase your channel's visibility and attract more viewers, it's important to promote your YouTube channel on other platforms and channels. Utilize social media, email newsletters, and your website to promote your videos and channel to your existing audience and beyond. Collaborate with other YouTubers or influencers in your niche to tap into their audience and gain more exposure. Participate in relevant online communities, forums, and groups to share your content and engage with potential viewers. The more you promote your channel, the more chances you have to grow your audience and increase your revenue potential.

Step 11: Stay Compliant with YouTube's Policies

It's crucial to always adhere to YouTube's policies and guidelines to maintain your monetization eligibility and avoid any issues that could jeopardize your revenue. Familiarize yourself with YouTube's community guidelines, copyright policies, and ad policies, and ensure that your content complies with them. Avoid any practices that could result in copyright infringement, spam, or other violations. Stay informed about any changes or updates to YouTube's policies and adjust your content and strategies accordingly to ensure long-term monetization success.

Step 12: Stay Motivated and Patient

Monetizing your YouTube channel takes time, effort, and patience. It's important to stay motivated and committed to creating high-quality content, engaging with your audience, and promoting your channel consistently. Success on YouTube doesn't happen overnight, and it's normal to face challenges and setbacks along the way. Stay positive, learn from your experiences, and keep pushing forward. Remember that with perseverance and dedication, you can achieve your goals of monetizing your YouTube channel and generating passive income.

By following these step-by-step instructions and implementing effective strategies, you can increase your chances of success in monetizing your YouTube channel and generating passive income. Remember that YouTube is a dynamic platform that constantly evolves, so it's crucial to stay updated with the latest trends, features, and policies. Keep learning, experimenting, and refining your content and strategies to stay ahead of the competition and keep growing your channel.

While YouTube monetization can offer a potential source of passive income, it's not a guaranteed overnight success. It may take time to build an audience, gain traction, and start earning significant revenue. Therefore, it's important to be patient, persistent, and resilient in your pursuit of monetizing your YouTube channel. With the right approach, mindset, and strategies, YouTube can be a powerful platform for marketers to generate passive income, build a loyal audience, and expand their digital marketing efforts.

Chapter 3

Optimizing Your Channel for Search and Discoverability

Creating a YouTube channel is just the first step towards making money on the platform. You also need to optimize your channel to ensure it is easily discoverable by your target audience. Here are some tips for optimizing your channel for search and discoverability:

1. Use Keywords: One of the most important ways to optimize your channel for search is to use keywords in your channel name, description, and tags. Use relevant keywords that describe your channel and the type of content you create.

2. Create Engaging Content: The more engaging your content, the higher the chances that viewers will spend more time on your channel. When viewers spend more time on your channel, it signals to YouTube that your content is valuable and relevant to your target audience, which can help your channel rank higher in search results.

3. Add Custom Thumbnails: Custom thumbnails can increase click-through rates and help your videos stand out in search results. Make sure to use high-quality images that accurately represent the content of your videos.

4. Use Descriptive Titles: Your video titles should accurately describe the content of your videos and include relevant keywords. Avoid using clickbait titles, as this can lead to viewers leaving your channel, which can negatively impact your search rankings.

5. Optimize Video Descriptions: Use your video descriptions to provide more context about your videos and include relevant keywords. Make sure to also include links to your social media profiles and website to drive traffic to your other online channels.

6. Utilize Tags: Tags can help your videos appear in YouTube's suggested videos section, which can increase views and watch time. Use relevant tags that accurately describe the content of your videos.

7. Engage with Your Audience: Engaging with your audience through comments and community posts can help build a loyal following and increase engagement on your channel. When viewers engage with your content, it signals to YouTube that your content is valuable, which can help improve your search rankings.

8. Promote Your Channel: Promote your channel on social media and other online platforms to increase visibility and drive traffic to your channel. The more traffic your channel receives, the more valuable it appears to YouTube's algorithm, which can help improve your search rankings.

9. Analyze Your Data: Use YouTube's analytics tools to monitor your channel's performance and make data-driven decisions about your content strategy. This can help you identify areas where you can improve your channel's search and discoverability.

Optimizing your channel for search and discoverability is an ongoing process that requires consistent effort and attention. By using relevant keywords, creating engaging content, and promoting your channel on social media and other online platforms, you can improve your channel's search rankings and increase your chances of making money on the platform.

Chapter 3

Importance of Branding and Consistency

When it comes to creating a successful YouTube channel, branding and consistency are two key elements that should not be overlooked. Branding refers to the visual and messaging identity that you create for your channel, while consistency is about maintaining a regular schedule of content and ensuring that your brand is reflected consistently across all platforms. In this chapter, we'll explore the importance of branding and consistency for your YouTube channel, and how you can implement these strategies to build a strong, recognizable brand that resonates with your audience.

First and foremost, branding helps establish your channel's identity and sets it apart from the competition. It encompasses everything from your channel name, logo, & color scheme, to the type of content you produce, and the tone and messaging used in your videos. Your brand should reflect the values and personality of your channel and be consistent across all your content and platforms. This will help viewers recognize and remember your channel, which can lead to increased engagement and growth.

Consistency is also crucial for building a successful YouTube channel. Viewers want to know what to expect from your channel and when to expect it. This means maintaining a regular upload schedule and ensuring that your content is consistently high quality and on-brand. By sticking to a regular schedule, you'll also help build anticipation and encourage viewers to return to your channel for new content.

Another benefit of branding and consistency is that it can help attract sponsorships and partnerships. Companies are more likely to work with channels that have a strong, recognizable brand and a consistent track record of producing high-quality content. By building a strong brand and maintaining a consistent schedule, you'll demonstrate to potential sponsors that you're serious about your channel and can deliver results.

To establish a strong brand, start by developing a clear mission statement and brand identity. Consider your target audience and what type of content they would be interested in. Develop a color scheme and logo that reflects your brand personality and use these consistently across all of your content and platforms. Ensure that your messaging and tone of voice are consistent across all of your content, from video titles and descriptions to social media posts and email newsletters.

Consistency can be achieved by developing a content calendar and sticking to a regular upload schedule. Consider the type of content your audience wants to see and how often you can realistically produce it. Be sure to also maintain consistency in your visual style and messaging, and use your branding elements consistently across all platforms.

In addition to branding and consistency, it's also important to monitor and respond to viewer feedback. Use analytics tools to track engagement and identify areas where you can improve your content and brand. Respond to comments and messages from viewers, and use this feedback to guide your content and branding decisions moving forward.

In summary, branding and consistency are essential for building a successful YouTube channel. They help establish your channel's identity and attract viewers, sponsorships, and partnerships. By developing a clear brand identity, maintaining a regular upload schedule, and responding to viewer feedback, you can build a strong, recognizable brand that resonates with your audience and sets your channel up for success.

Chapter 4: Finding Profitable Niche Markets

Chapter 4

Importance of Finding a Profitable Niche

One of the crucial factors for success on YouTube is finding a profitable niche. A niche is a specialized topic or area of interest that has a dedicated and engaged audience. By focusing on a profitable niche, you can create content that resonates with your target audience, drives engagement, and generates revenue. In this chapter, we'll delve into the importance of finding a profitable niche for your YouTube channel and how it can significantly impact your success as a content creator.

Finding a profitable niche allows you to target a specific audience with a focused and tailored approach. When you create content that caters to the interests, needs, and preferences of a particular niche, you are more likely to attract viewers who are genuinely interested in your content. This leads to higher engagement, longer watch times, and increased loyalty among your audience.

A profitable niche provides an opportunity to differentiate yourself from the competition. With millions of videos uploaded to YouTube every day, standing out can be challenging. However, by choosing a niche that is not overly saturated, you can carve out a unique position for your channel and establish yourself as an authority in that specific area. This can lead to increased visibility, brand recognition, and ultimately, more revenue-generating opportunities.

Another significant advantage of finding a profitable niche is the potential for monetization. When you create content that caters to a specific audience, you are more likely to attract advertisers and sponsors who are interested in reaching that specific demographic. This can open opportunities for brand partnerships, sponsored content, and other revenue streams that can help you generate income from your YouTube channel.

Additionally, a profitable niche allows you to build a dedicated and engaged community. When you create content that resonates with your audience's interests, they are more likely to become loyal followers and engage with your content through comments, likes, and shares. This not only boosts your channel's engagement metrics, but it also fosters a sense of community and connection among your viewers, which can further enhance your channel's success.

To find a profitable niche, start by conducting thorough research. Identify topics or areas of interest that have a dedicated and engaged audience but are not overly saturated with content. Consider your own passions, skills, and expertise, and look for opportunities to create content that aligns with those areas. Use YouTube's search and trending features, as well as social media and other online platforms, to identify popular niches and trending topics.

Once you've identified a niche, conduct competitor analysis to understand what others are doing in that space and how you can differentiate yourself. Look for gaps or opportunities that you can fill with your unique content and perspective. Develop a clear content strategy that aligns with your niche and audience, and create high-quality, engaging content that provides value to your viewers.

Consistency is key in building a successful channel in a profitable niche. Establish a regular upload schedule and stick to it, so your audience knows when to expect new content from you. Engage with your viewers and encourage feedback to better understand their needs and preferences. Stay up to date with industry trends and adapt your content strategy accordingly to stay relevant and continue providing value to your audience.

There are many tools and resources available that can help you find a profitable niche for your YouTube channel. By using these tools and resources, you can identify a profitable niche for your YouTube channel and create content that resonates with your target audience. Remember, the key is to provide value and solve problems for your viewers, so choose a niche that you are passionate about and that you can create great content for. Here are some of the most popular ones:

1. Google Trends: This free tool from Google lets you see how popular a particular search term has been over time. You can use it to find trends in your niche and see what topics are currently popular.
2. YouTube Search Bar: This is a simple but effective way to find out what people are searching for on YouTube. Start typing in a keyword related to your niche, and YouTube will suggest related search terms that people are currently using.
3. Social Media: Social media platforms like Facebook, Twitter, and Instagram can be great sources of information about your target audience. Look for groups and pages related to your niche and see what topics people are discussing.
4. Keyword Research Tools: Tools like Google Keyword Planner, Ubersuggest, and SEMrush can help you identify high-volume keywords and phrases related to your niche.

You can use this information to create content that is optimized for search engines.

5. Amazon: Amazon is a great resource for finding popular products and niches. Look for best-seller lists and customer reviews to see what people are currently buying and what they are interested in.

6. Online Forums: Online forums like Reddit and Quora are great places to see what questions people have about your niche. You can use this information to create content that answers these questions and provides value to your audience.

7. Competitor Analysis: Look at the channels that are already successful in your niche and see what they are doing. Analyze their content, their branding, and their marketing strategies to see what works and what doesn't.

Finding a profitable niche is crucial for building a successful YouTube channel. It allows you to target a specific audience, differentiate yourself from the competition, monetize your content, and build a dedicated community. By conducting thorough research, developing a clear content strategy, and consistently delivering high-quality content, you can position your channel for success and unlock the potential for revenue generation on the YouTube platform.

Chapter 4

Tips for Researching Potential Niches

When it comes to creating a successful YouTube channel, choosing the right niche is crucial. A niche is a specific topic or subject that your channel will focus on, and it's important to research potential niches thoroughly to ensure they are profitable and have the potential to attract and engage your target audience. Here are some tips for researching potential niches for your YouTube channel:

1. Identify your passions and interests: The first step in researching potential niches is to identify your own passions and interests. Think about topics that you are genuinely interested in and knowledgeable about, as this will help you create content that you are passionate about and that resonates with your audience.

2. Conduct market research: Research the market demand for potential niches by using tools like Google Trends, YouTube Search Bar, and social media platforms. Look for niches that have a growing demand and are not oversaturated with existing content.

3. Analyze competitor channels: Look at existing YouTube channels that cover similar topics to the niches you are considering. Analyze their content, audience engagement, and subscriber base to understand what is already working in that niche and what gaps you can fill with your own content.

4. Consider target audience demographics: Think about the demographics of your target audience, such as age, gender, location, and interests. Choose a niche that aligns with the

preferences and interests of your ideal audience to ensure your content will resonate with them.

5. Evaluate monetization potential: Consider the potential for monetization in each niche. Research if there are opportunities for sponsorship deals, affiliate marketing, or other revenue streams in that niche. Look for niches that have a high potential for monetization to help you generate income from your YouTube channel.

6. Research content ideas: Brainstorm content ideas for each potential niche to ensure that you will have a steady stream of content to create. Look for niches that have a wide range of content ideas and that you can consistently create engaging and valuable content for.

7. Assess long-term sustainability: Consider the long-term sustainability of each potential niche. Look for niches that are not likely to fade away quickly or become outdated, but rather have a lasting appeal and potential for growth in the future.

8. Evaluate competition: Consider the level of competition in each niche. While some competition can be healthy, choosing a niche that is highly competitive may make it harder for your channel to stand out. Look for niches where you can differentiate yourself and provide unique value to your audience.

9. Assess scalability: Consider the scalability of each potential niche. Look for niches that have the potential for growth and expansion beyond YouTube, such as through related products, services, or online communities.

10. Test audience interest: Test the interest of your target audience in each potential niche by creating a pilot video or conducting surveys and polls. Get feedback from your

target audience to see if they are interested in the content you plan to create and if it resonates with them.

11. Consider your expertise: Evaluate your own expertise and ability to create high-quality content in each potential niche. Choose niches where you have the knowledge, skills, and passion to create content that stands out and provides value to your audience.

12. Think about your long-term goals: Consider your long-term goals for your YouTube channel and how each potential niche aligns with those goals. Choose niches that are in line with your overall vision and can help you achieve your goals for your channel and your business.

13. Stay true to your brand: Consider how each potential niche aligns with your personal brand and the brand image you want to project on YouTube. Choose niches that are consistent with your brand values, personality, and style.

14. Think about audience engagement: Consider the potential for audience engagement in each niche. Look for niches where you can create content that encourages audience interaction, such as through comments, likes, shares, and discussions. Niches that have a passionate and engaged audience are more likely to attract loyal followers and build a community around your channel.

15. Keep an eye on trends: Stay updated with the latest trends and topics in your industry or niche. Look for niches that are currently gaining popularity or have the potential to become popular in the future. Creating content around trending topics can help you attract more viewers and stay relevant in a fast-paced digital landscape.

16. Evaluate keyword search volume: Use keyword research tools to evaluate the search volume and competition for

relevant keywords in each potential niche. Look for niches that have a decent search volume but are not overly competitive, as this can help you optimize your content for SEO and improve your channel's discoverability.

17. Consider platform policies: Familiarize yourself with the platform policies and guidelines of YouTube. Make sure that your potential niche aligns with YouTube's terms of service, community guidelines, and copyright policies. Choosing a niche that violates YouTube's policies can result in your channel being flagged or even terminated, which can be detrimental to your long-term success.

18. Assess your resources: Consider the resources you have available to create content for each potential niche. Evaluate your time, budget, equipment, and team (if applicable) to ensure that you can consistently produce high-quality content in the niche you choose. Niches that require extensive resources or expertise may not be feasible for beginners or those with limited resources.

19. Trust your intuition: As a creator, you have a unique perspective and understanding of your own strengths and interests. Trust your intuition and gut feeling. Choose a niche that aligns with your intuition and excitement, as this will motivate you to create the best content possible and stay committed to your channel in the long run.

Researching potential niches is a critical step in building a successful YouTube channel. Finding the right niche is the foundation of a successful YouTube channel, and it's worth taking the time and effort to research and choose the right one that aligns with your goals, interests, and target audience.

Chapter 4

Evaluating Profit Potential

When it comes to monetizing your YouTube channel, evaluating the profit potential of your content is a crucial step. While creating engaging and valuable content is essential, understanding how to generate revenue from your channel is equally important. Here are key factors to consider when evaluating the profit potential of your YouTube channel.

1. Audience size and engagement: The size and engagement of your audience play a significant role in determining your profit potential. A larger and more engaged audience is likely to generate more views, likes, comments, shares, and ultimately more revenue. Analyze your channel's metrics, such as subscriber count, view count, watch time, and audience demographics, to understand the size and engagement of your audience and how it can impact your profit potential.

2. Ad revenue: YouTube's Partner Program allows creators to earn money through ad revenue from ads displayed on their videos. Ad revenue is primarily generated based on the number of views and clicks on the ads. Consider the types of ads that are relevant to your content and target audience, as well as the average CPM (cost per thousand views) in your niche, to estimate your potential ad revenue.

3. Affiliate marketing: Another way to generate revenue is through affiliate marketing, where you promote products or services in your videos and earn a commission for each sale or click made through your affiliate links. Evaluate

the potential for relevant affiliate partnerships in your niche and the earning potential based on the products or services you can promote to your audience.

4. Sponsored content: Collaborating with brands and creating sponsored content can be a profitable avenue for generating revenue. Consider the potential for sponsored content based on your niche, audience size, and engagement. Assess the market rates for sponsored content in your niche and the potential for long-term partnerships to estimate your earning potential.

5. Merchandise sales: If you have a dedicated fan base, you may consider selling merchandise related to your content, such as branded merchandise, merchandise with your logo, or products related to your niche. Evaluate the demand for merchandise sales in your niche and the potential for generating revenue through merchandise sales.

6. Crowdfunding: Crowdfunding platforms such as Patreon or Kickstarter allow creators to generate revenue by accepting direct contributions from their audience in exchange for exclusive content or perks. Assess the potential for crowdfunding based on your content and audience engagement and consider incorporating crowdfunding into your monetization strategy.

7. Product or service creation: Depending on your niche, you may have the opportunity to create and sell your own products or services related to your content. For example, if you are a fitness YouTuber, you may create and sell a fitness program or merchandise. Evaluate the demand and potential profitability of creating and selling your own products or services.

8. Sponsorship opportunities: Apart from sponsored content, there may be other opportunities for sponsorships, such as event sponsorships, speaking engagements, or brand partnerships. Research and assess the potential for such opportunities in your niche and consider incorporating them into your monetization strategy.

9. Market demand and competition: Evaluate the market demand and competition for your niche to understand the profit potential. Is there a high demand for content in your niche? Are there other successful channels in your niche? Understanding the market dynamics and competition can help you assess the profit potential of your channel and identify areas where you can differentiate and excel.

10. Long-term sustainability: Consider the long-term sustainability of your monetization strategy. Will the revenue streams you have identified be sustainable in the long run? Are there potential risks or challenges that may impact your profit potential in the future? Assessing the long-term sustainability of your monetization strategy can help you make informed decisions and set realistic expectations.

11. Diversification of revenue streams: It's essential to diversify your revenue streams to minimize risks and maximize your profit potential. Relying solely on one revenue stream, such as ad revenue, can be risky as it may fluctuate based on factors beyond your control, such as changes in YouTube's policies or ad market conditions. Evaluate the potential for multiple revenue streams, such as affiliate marketing, sponsored content, merchandise sales, crowdfunding, and product or service creation, to create a diverse and sustainable monetization strategy.

12. Cost and effort involved: Evaluate the cost and effort involved in implementing your monetization strategy. Some revenue streams may require upfront investments, such as merchandise creation or product development, while others may require ongoing efforts, such as affiliate marketing or sponsored content. Consider the time, resources, and skills required to implement each revenue stream and assess whether it aligns with your overall goals and capabilities.

13. Audience feedback and engagement: Pay attention to your audience's feedback and engagement with your content. Are they actively engaged with your videos, leaving comments, sharing your content, and expressing interest in your monetization efforts? Audience feedback and engagement can be an indicator of your content's relevance and potential for generating revenue. Consider incorporating feedback from your audience into your monetization strategy to align with their preferences and interests.

14. Trends and opportunities: Stay updated with the latest trends and opportunities in your niche and the overall YouTube ecosystem. Identifying emerging trends or opportunities, such as new content formats, popular keywords, or changes in user behavior, can give you a competitive edge and help you capitalize on potential profit-generating opportunities. Stay proactive and adaptable in your approach to monetization to stay ahead of the curve and optimize your profit potential.

15. Experimentation and optimization: Monetization strategies may require experimentation and optimization over time. It's important to be open to trying different

approaches, analyzing the results, and adjusting accordingly. Track and analyze the performance of your revenue streams and iterate on your strategies to optimize your profit potential. Remember that monetization on YouTube is not a one-size-fits-all approach, and what works for one channel may not work for another. Be willing to learn, adapt, and optimize your monetization strategy based on your unique audience, niche, and content.

In conclusion, evaluating the profit potential of your YouTube channel is a crucial step in building a successful monetization strategy. By thoroughly evaluating these factors and aligning your monetization strategy with your audience and niche, you can maximize your profit potential and create a sustainable source of income from your YouTube channel.

Chapter 4

Strategies for Identifying Gaps in the Market

As a YouTube creator, identifying gaps in the market is a key step in building a successful and profitable channel. By finding niches or areas that are not fully explored or catered to, you can create content that fills those gaps and attracts a dedicated audience. Here are some key strategies for identifying gaps in the market that can help you stand out and thrive on YouTube.

1. Research competitor channels: Start by researching the existing channels in your niche or industry. Analyze their content, engagement, and audience. Look for gaps or areas that are not fully covered or addressed in their content. Pay attention to the comments section and social media channels of these competitors to see what their audience is asking for or what needs are not being met. This can give you insights into potential gaps in the market that you can capitalize on.

2. Keyword research: Utilize keyword research tools to identify popular keywords and search queries related to your niche. Look for keywords with a decent search volume but relatively low competition. These keywords can indicate potential gaps in the market that are not fully addressed in existing content. You can create content around these keywords and target those gaps to attract a unique audience that is searching for that specific content.

3. Analyze audience feedback: Pay attention to the feedback and comments from your own audience or from other content creators' audiences in your niche. Look for

common questions, complaints, or requests for specific content that are not being addressed. This can give you insights into gaps in the market that you can fill with your content. Engage with your audience through comments, surveys, or social media to gather feedback and understand their needs better.

4. Explore related niches: Consider exploring related niches or industries that are relevant to your content. Look for areas within those niches that are not fully covered or have limited content. For example, if you have a channel about fitness, you can explore related niches such as nutrition, mental health, or workout gear, and identify gaps in those areas. This can open up new opportunities for content creation and monetization.

5. Stay updated with trends: Stay updated with the latest trends, news, and events in your niche or industry. Look for emerging trends or topics that are gaining traction but have limited content available. By staying ahead of the curve, you can identify gaps in the market and create content that addresses those trends. This can help you attract a growing audience and gain a competitive advantage.

6. Conduct surveys or polls: Conducting surveys or polls among your audience or in relevant online communities can be a valuable strategy to identify gaps in the market. Ask your audience about their preferences, needs, and content they wish to see more of. You can also seek feedback from relevant online communities or forums to understand what type of content is missing or needed. This can provide you with valuable insights and ideas for creating content that fills those gaps.

7. Utilize analytics and data: Utilize analytics and data to identify gaps in the market. Analyze the performance of your existing content and look for patterns or trends. Identify content that performs well and content that underperforms. Look for gaps in your content library where there may be room for improvement or additional content. Utilize YouTube analytics, Google Analytics, or other data tools to gain insights into audience behavior and preferences and identify potential gaps in the market.

8. Be a problem solver: One effective approach to identifying gaps in the market is to be a problem solver. Think about the pain points, challenges, or unanswered questions your target audience may have, and create content that addresses those issues. By providing solutions, tips, or insights on topics that are not well covered, you can attract an audience that is actively seeking solutions to their problems. Being a problem solver can help you establish yourself as an authority in your niche and build a loyal audience.

9. Pay attention to audience engagement: Pay close attention to the engagement metrics of your content, such as likes, comments, shares, and views. Look for patterns or trends in the content that receives higher engagement. This can indicate that you are hitting on topics or angles that resonate with your audience and are filling gaps in the market. Take note of the content that generates the most engagement and try to create more content that follows a similar pattern.

10. Be unique and authentic: Don't be afraid to be unique and authentic in your content. Embrace your own personality, perspective, and style to differentiate yourself from other

content creators in your niche. Avoid copying or replicating content that already exists in the market. Instead, focus on creating content that is truly unique, original, and authentic. This can help you stand out and fill gaps in the market with your fresh perspective and approach.

11. Follow your passion: When identifying gaps in the market, it's important to follow your passion and interests. Creating content in a niche that you are genuinely interested in and passionate about can give you the motivation and drive to consistently produce high-quality content. It's easier to identify gaps in the market and create unique content when you are genuinely interested and knowledgeable about the subject matter.

12. Keep an eye on competition: While it's important to avoid copying or replicating content from competitors, it's also crucial to keep an eye on your competition to identify gaps in the market. Analyze their content, engagement, and audience to see if there are any areas that are not fully addressed or gaps that you can fill with your content. By staying informed about your competition, you can identify opportunities to create content that is unique and provides value to your audience.

13. Experiment with different content types and formats: Another strategy for identifying gaps in the market is to experiment with different types of content formats. Try different formats such as tutorials, reviews, vlogs, interviews, or behind-the-scenes content to see which ones resonate the most with your audience. You may discover that certain formats are not well covered in your niche, and you can fill those gaps by creating content in those

formats. Experimenting with different content types and formats can help you uncover new opportunities and cater to a wider audience.

14. Consider demographics and psychographics: Consider the demographics and psychographics of your target audience when identifying gaps in the market. Demographics such as age, gender, location, and interests can help you identify content gaps that are specific to certain segments of your audience. Psychographics such as values, beliefs, and behaviors can also provide insights into content gaps that align with the preferences and needs of your target audience. By understanding the demographics and psychographics of your audience, you can create content that resonates with them and fills gaps in the market.

15. Keep an open mind and adapt: Finally, keep an open mind and be willing to adapt your content strategy based on feedback, data, and changing market trends. The YouTube platform and the digital landscape are constantly evolving, and it's important to stay flexible and adaptable. Be open to feedback from your audience, monitor data and analytics, and stay updated with the latest trends and changes in your niche. By being adaptive and responsive, you can identify and fill gaps in the market as they arise and stay ahead of the competition.

Identifying gaps in the market is a critical strategy for success on the YouTube platform. Stay positive, persistent, and adaptive in your approach, and continue to refine your content strategy as you navigate the ever-evolving landscape of YouTube. With the right strategies and mindset, you can establish yourself as a successful content creator, generate passive income, and thrive on the YouTube platform.

Chapter 5: Monetizing Your Channel with Affiliate Marketing

Chapter 5

How Affiliate Marketing Works on YouTube

Affiliate marketing is a popular and effective way to monetize your YouTube channel and generate passive income. Let's dive in and explore how affiliate marketing works on YouTube, and how you can leverage this strategy to create a successful money-making machine on the platform.

Affiliate marketing is a form of performance-based marketing where you promote products or services of other companies and earn a commission for every sale or action that is generated through your referral. YouTube is a powerful platform for affiliate marketing due to its vast user base, high engagement levels, and ability to create compelling visual content.

To get started with affiliate marketing on YouTube, you need to first join an affiliate program. There are numerous affiliate programs available across various niches and industries, ranging from e-commerce and digital products to travel and lifestyle. Some popular affiliate programs include Amazon Associates, ShareASale, Commission Junction, and ClickBank. Choose an affiliate program that aligns with your niche and target audience and sign up for an account.

Once you have joined an affiliate program, you can start creating content on YouTube that incorporates your affiliate links. This can be in the form of product reviews, tutorials, demonstrations, or recommendations. The key is to create authentic and valuable content that resonates with your audience and provides them with valuable information about the products or services you are promoting.

When creating content for affiliate marketing, it's crucial to disclose that you are using affiliate links and that you may earn a commission for any purchases made through your links. This is important to comply with Federal Trade Commission (FTC) guidelines and maintain transparency with your audience.

Incorporating your affiliate links strategically is essential for success in affiliate marketing on YouTube. You can place your affiliate links in your video descriptions, annotations, or even in your video itself through verbal or visual call-to-actions. Be sure to use relevant and compelling calls-to-action that encourage your viewers to click on your affiliate links and make a purchase.

It's important to choose products or services that are relevant to your niche and audience. Avoid promoting products solely for the sake of earning a commission, as this can undermine your credibility and trust with your audience. Focus on products or services that you genuinely believe in and that align with the interests and needs of your viewers.

Tracking your affiliate marketing efforts is crucial to understanding your performance and optimizing your strategy. Most affiliate programs provide tracking and reporting tools that allow you to monitor your clicks, conversions, and earnings. Use these tools to analyze your performance, identify what is working, and make data-driven decisions to improve your results.

Building a relationship with your audience is key to successful affiliate marketing on YouTube. Engage with your viewers in the comments section, respond to their questions, and build a community around your content. By establishing trust and rapport with your audience, you can increase their likelihood of clicking on your affiliate links and making a purchase.

Experiment with different types of affiliate marketing content to see what resonates best with your audience. This can include product reviews, tutorials, comparisons, unboxings, and more. Pay attention to the feedback and engagement you receive from your audience and adjust your content accordingly to optimize your results.

Be patient and persistent in your affiliate marketing efforts on YouTube. It takes time to build an audience, gain their trust, and generate significant affiliate commissions. Don't get discouraged if you don't see immediate results. Stay consistent with your content creation, continue to optimize your strategy based on data and feedback, and keep refining your approach to maximize your earnings.

Affiliate marketing on YouTube can be a game-changer for marketers who want to monetize their channel and generate passive income. It requires strategic planning, consistent effort, and a deep understanding of your audience's needs and preferences. By following the tips and strategies outlined in this section, you can build a successful YouTube money-making machine through affiliate marketing.

Remember, it's essential to always prioritize providing value to your audience and maintaining transparency in your promotions. With determination, persistence, and a commitment to continuous improvement, you can achieve financial success through affiliate marketing on YouTube and turn your channel into a profitable online business. So, keep learning, experimenting, and refining your approach, and get ready to reap the rewards of your hard work and dedication. The possibilities are endless when it comes to affiliate marketing on YouTube, and the potential for earning passive income is only limited by your creativity and effort.

Chapter 5

Selecting Affiliate Products to Promote

Affiliate marketing is a powerful way to monetize your YouTube channel and generate passive income. By partnering with affiliate programs and promoting their products or services, you can earn a commission for each sale or action that is generated through your referral link. However, to be successful with affiliate marketing on YouTube, it's crucial to select the right affiliate products to promote. Here are key strategies and considerations for selecting affiliate products that are aligned with your channel's content, audience, and goals.

1. Know Your Audience: The first step in selecting affiliate products to promote on YouTube is to have a deep understanding of your audience. Who are they? What are their interests, preferences, and pain points? What types of products or services would they find valuable or relevant? By knowing your audience inside out, you can identify affiliate products that align with their needs and preferences, increasing the chances of generating sales and commissions.

2. Align with Your Channel's Content: It's crucial to promote affiliate products that are aligned with your channel's content. The products you promote should complement and enhance the content you create, rather than feeling forced or out of place. For example, if you have a fitness channel, promoting fitness equipment, supplements, or workout programs would be relevant. Promoting products that are unrelated or irrelevant to your content can erode

your audience's trust and credibility, ultimately affecting your affiliate marketing success.

3. Research Affiliate Programs: Conduct thorough research to identify reputable and trustworthy affiliate programs that offer products or services that align with your niche and audience. Look for programs with a proven track record of providing reliable tracking, timely payments, and good commission rates. Consider factors such as the product's quality, reputation, and customer satisfaction to ensure that you are promoting products that add value to your audience and align with your brand.

4. Test the Products: It's important to test the products or services yourself before promoting them. This allows you to provide honest and accurate reviews or recommendations to your audience, which can build trust and credibility. Testing the products also helps you understand their features, benefits, and limitations, allowing you to create more informative and persuasive content that resonates with your audience.

5. Consider Commission Rates and Payment Terms: When selecting affiliate products to promote, consider the commission rates and payment terms offered by the affiliate program. Commission rates vary depending on the product or service, and it's important to choose products that offer fair and competitive commissions. Also, review the payment terms, such as the frequency of payments and the minimum payout threshold, to ensure they align with your expectations and financial goals.

6. Check for Seasonality and Trends: Consider the seasonality and trends of the products or services you plan to promote. Some products may have higher demand

during specific seasons or events, while others may have consistent demand throughout the year. Stay updated with industry trends and market demand to ensure you are promoting products that are relevant and appealing to your audience.

7. Evaluate Product Performance: Assess the performance of the products you promote over time. Track the sales, conversion rates, and earnings generated from each product to determine their effectiveness. Consider factors such as the product's popularity, user feedback, and customer satisfaction to make informed decisions about which products to continue promoting and which ones to discontinue.

8. Consider Affiliate Marketing Policies and Guidelines: Different affiliate programs may have varying policies and guidelines that you need to adhere to when promoting their products. Familiarize yourself with these policies and guidelines to ensure that your promotions comply with the program's rules and regulations. Violating affiliate marketing policies can result in the termination of your affiliate account and loss of commissions.

9. Disclose Affiliate Relationships: Transparency is crucial in affiliate marketing. Be sure to disclose your affiliate relationships to your audience clearly and prominently in your videos or descriptions. Disclosing your affiliate relationships helps build trust with your audience and ensures compliance with Federal Trade Commission (FTC) regulations regarding affiliate marketing disclosures. Clearly state that you may earn a commission when viewers make purchases through your affiliate links

and provide honest and unbiased reviews or recommendations.

10. Consider Your Channel's Brand and Values: Your YouTube channel has its own unique brand and values, and it's important to consider these when selecting affiliate products to promote. Ensure that the products you promote align with your channel's brand image, values, and overall messaging. Consistency in brand and values helps build trust with your audience and reinforces your channel's authenticity.

11. Look for Additional Value for Your Audience: Seek affiliate products that provide additional value to your audience beyond just a commission. For example, products that offer exclusive discounts, bonuses, or special promotions for your viewers can be enticing and increase the likelihood of conversions. Look for ways to provide extra value to your audience through the products you promote, as it can strengthen your relationship with them.

12. Consider Customer Support and Returns: Consider the customer support and returns policy of the products or services you promote. It's important to promote products from affiliate programs that offer reliable and responsive customer support, as this reflects on your credibility as an affiliate marketer. Additionally, consider the return policy of the products to ensure that your audience is protected in case they are not satisfied with their purchase.

13. Evaluate Competition and Market Saturation: Assess the competition and market saturation for the affiliate products you plan to promote. High competition or market saturation can make it challenging to generate sales and commissions, as there may be numerous other affiliates

promoting the same products to the same audience. Consider targeting niche or unique products that have lower competition, as it can increase your chances of success.

14. Consider Long-term Potential: While it's important to generate short-term commissions from affiliate products, also consider their long-term potential. Look for products that have a recurring commission structure, subscription-based models, or upsell opportunities that can generate ongoing revenue. Building a sustainable and long-term affiliate marketing strategy can provide consistent passive income for your YouTube channel.

15. Continuously Review and Update Your Affiliate Products: Affiliate marketing is not a one-time setup, but an ongoing process. Continuously review and update the affiliate products you promote to ensure they are still relevant, effective, and aligned with your channel's goals and audience. Stay updated with industry trends, customer feedback, and changes in affiliate program policies to make informed decisions and optimize your affiliate marketing strategy.

Affiliate marketing on YouTube can be a profitable venture when approached strategically, with a focus on providing value to your audience, building trust, and staying updated with the latest industry trends. It is not a one-time effort, but an ongoing process that requires consistent effort and adaptation. Embrace a growth mindset and be open to testing and trying new approaches to optimize your results.

Chapter 5

Creating Effective Affiliate Marketing Campaigns

Affiliate marketing on YouTube can be a powerful way to monetize your channel and generate passive income. However, to maximize your earnings and create successful campaigns, it's important to approach affiliate marketing strategically and create effective campaigns that resonate with your audience.

1. Identify Your Target Audience: Before you start promoting affiliate products, it's crucial to identify and understand your target audience. Who are they? What are their interests, preferences, and pain points? Conduct thorough research to gain insights into your audience's demographics, interests, and behavior. This information will help you choose the right affiliate products that align with your audience's needs and preferences.

2. Choose Relevant Affiliate Products: Selecting the right affiliate products is critical to the success of your campaign. Choose products that are relevant to your niche and audience. Consider the quality, reputation, and relevance of the products to ensure they align with your content and audience's interests. Avoid promoting products solely for the sake of earning a commission, as this can undermine your credibility and trust with your audience.

3. Provide Value and Authenticity: Creating valuable and authentic content is key to building trust with your audience. Avoid overtly promoting products in a salesy manner. Instead, focus on providing genuine value and insights about the products you are promoting. Share your

personal experiences, reviews, and recommendations to establish authenticity and credibility with your audience. This will help you build trust, which is crucial for successful affiliate marketing campaigns.

4. Create Compelling Call-to-Actions (CTAs): Your CTAs play a critical role in motivating your audience to take action. Create compelling CTAs that encourage your audience to click on your affiliate links or make a purchase. Use persuasive language, clear instructions, and a sense of urgency to prompt your audience to take action. Experiment with different CTAs and track their performance to optimize your campaigns for better results.

5. Leverage Different Types of Content: YouTube offers various content formats, including tutorials, reviews, comparisons, hauls, and more. Experiment with different types of content to promote your affiliate products. For example, you can create in-depth product reviews, tutorials showcasing the product's features and benefits, or even share personal stories and experiences related to the products. Use engaging visuals, compelling storytelling, and high-quality production value to captivate your audience.

6. Optimize Your Videos for Search: YouTube is a search engine, and optimizing your videos for search can significantly boost your visibility and reach. Conduct keyword research to identify relevant keywords and incorporate them in your video titles, descriptions, tags, and captions. This will help your videos rank higher in YouTube search results and increase the chances of attracting organic traffic.

7. Build Relationships with Affiliate Partners: Building relationships with your affiliate partners can be beneficial in the long run. Maintain open communication, seek feedback, and stay updated with their product launches, promotions, and updates. Some affiliates may offer exclusive deals, promotions, or bonuses for their partners, which can give you an edge in your campaigns. Building a strong relationship with your affiliate partners can also lead to future collaborations and increased earning potential.

8. Track and Analyze Your Campaigns: Monitoring and analyzing the performance of your campaigns is crucial to optimize your results. Use YouTube analytics, affiliate program analytics, and other tracking tools to assess the performance of your campaigns. Track key metrics such as click-through rates (CTR), conversion rates, earnings per click (EPC), and overall revenue. Identify patterns, trends, and areas of improvement to make data-driven decisions and optimize your campaigns for better results.

9. Stay Compliant with Affiliate Marketing Rules: It's important to adhere to the rules and policies of the affiliate programs you participate in. Familiarize yourself with the terms and conditions of the affiliate programs, and ensure that you are compliant with their guidelines. Avoid using deceptive or misleading tactics, such as false claims or exaggerated promises, in your promotions. Be transparent with your audience about your affiliate partnerships and disclose your affiliate links according to the relevant regulations and guidelines. Building a trustworthy and compliant affiliate marketing strategy will help you

establish a positive reputation and maintain the trust of your audience.

Creating effective affiliate marketing campaigns on YouTube requires a strategic approach, focused on understanding your audience, providing value and authenticity. It takes dedication, consistency, and continuous improvement to achieve your financial goals through affiliate marketing on YouTube. With the right approach and mindset, you can turn your YouTube channel into a profitable money-making machine through effective affiliate marketing campaigns.

Chapter 5

Disclosing Affiliate Relationships and Maintaining Trust

As an affiliate marketer on YouTube, it's crucial to prioritize transparency and maintain the trust of your audience. Disclosing your affiliate relationships and being authentic in your recommendations can build a loyal following and contribute to your long-term success.

Transparency is key in affiliate marketing on YouTube. It's important to disclose your affiliate relationships clearly and prominently in your videos, descriptions, and other relevant platforms. Your audience should be aware that you may receive a commission or other compensation when they make a purchase through your affiliate links. Disclosing your affiliate relationships upfront shows integrity and establishes trust with your audience, as it demonstrates that you are being honest and transparent about your motives for promoting products or services.

When disclosing your affiliate relationships, be clear and concise. Use clear and easily understandable language to explain that you may earn a commission or receive compensation for the products or services you recommend. Avoid using small or hard-to-read disclaimers buried in the fine print. Disclosures should be prominent and easily noticeable, such as in the video description, in a pop-up message, or as a verbal disclosure in the video itself.

In addition to disclosing your affiliate relationships, it's important to maintain trust with your audience through authenticity. Authenticity is the foundation of building a loyal following on YouTube. Your audience expects genuine recommendations and honest opinions from you as an affiliate marketer. Avoid making exaggerated claims or endorsing products solely for the sake of earning commissions. Instead, focus on products or services that genuinely align with your values, interests, and expertise, and that you believe will bring value to your audience.

Being transparent about potential biases or conflicts of interest is also important in maintaining trust with your audience. If you have a personal or financial relationship with the products or services you are promoting, it's essential to disclose that information to your audience. For example, if you have received free products or services, have a close relationship with the brand or its representatives, or have any other financial or personal incentives, it's important to disclose that information clearly to avoid any perception of bias.

Regularly reviewing and updating your disclosures is also essential. As your channel grows and your affiliate partnerships evolve, it's crucial to revisit your disclosures and ensure they are up-to-date and accurate. Keep yourself informed about the latest guidelines and regulations regarding affiliate marketing, as they may change over time. Staying compliant with the rules and regulations demonstrates your professionalism as an affiliate marketer and builds trust with your audience.

In addition to disclosures, building a strong relationship with your audience through engagement and communication is crucial. Respond to comments, messages, and inquiries from your audience promptly and respectfully. Encourage feedback, questions, and discussions related to the products or services you promote. Engaging with your audience fosters a sense of community & trust, and shows that you value their opinions and feedback.

Finally, be cautious about the products or services you promote and avoid promoting low-quality or unethical products that may damage your reputation and erode your audience's trust. Research and thoroughly evaluate the products or services you are considering promoting to ensure they are of high quality, reputable, and align with your values and audience's interests. Consider the potential impact on your audience's well-being and always prioritize their best interests.

Disclosing affiliate relationships and maintaining trust with your audience is paramount in affiliate marketing on YouTube. Transparency, authenticity, regular review of disclosures, engagement with your audience, and careful product selection are essential elements of building a successful and sustainable affiliate marketing strategy. By prioritizing trust and maintaining open and honest communication with your audience, you can establish a loyal following, foster a positive reputation, and achieve long-term success as an affiliate marketer on YouTube.

Chapter 6: Monetizing Your Channel with Sponsorships

Chapter 6

How Sponsorships Work on YouTube

As a content creator on YouTube, one of the potential revenue streams you can explore is sponsorships. Sponsorships are partnerships between YouTubers and brands, where creators promote products or services in their videos in exchange for compensation. Let's take a dive into how sponsorships work on YouTube and how you can leverage them to monetize your content and grow your YouTube money-making machine.

1. Understanding Sponsorships: Sponsorships are a form of influencer marketing, where brands collaborate with YouTubers to promote their products or services. This can be in the form of product reviews, endorsements, testimonials, tutorials, or branded content. Brands often approach YouTubers who have a significant and engaged audience that aligns with their target market. In exchange for promoting the brand's product or service, YouTubers receive compensation, which can be in the form of cash, free products, or other perks.

2. Finding Sponsorship Opportunities: There are several ways to find sponsorship opportunities on YouTube. One common approach is to wait for brands to reach out to you directly. However, it's also proactive to seek out potential sponsors by researching relevant brands in your niche, reaching out to them with a compelling pitch, and showcasing the value you can offer as a YouTuber. Another option is to join influencer marketing platforms that connect YouTubers with brands looking for sponsorships. These platforms streamline the process of

finding and securing sponsorships and often offer additional benefits such as payment protection and contract management.

3. Negotiating Sponsorship Deals: When it comes to negotiating sponsorship deals, it's essential to consider factors such as your channel's size, engagement, niche, and the brand's budget. Be prepared to discuss the scope of work, compensation, timeline, and any specific requirements or guidelines set by the brand. It's crucial to maintain transparency and clear communication throughout the negotiation process to ensure that both parties are aligned and satisfied with the terms of the deal.

4. Disclosing Sponsored Content: Transparency is key in sponsorship deals. As a YouTuber, it's crucial to disclose sponsored content to your audience. This can be done through verbal disclosures in your videos, visible text disclosures in video descriptions or captions, and by following YouTube's guidelines on sponsored content disclosures. Disclosing sponsored content helps maintain trust with your audience and ensures compliance with legal regulations and YouTube's policies.

5. Creating Authentic Sponsored Content: To create effective sponsored content, it's important to prioritize authenticity. Your audience expects genuine and honest opinions from you as a content creator. Avoid being overly promotional or endorsing products that don't align with your values or your audience's interests. Instead, focus on creating engaging and informative content that provides value to your viewers while integrating the brand's message or product in a seamless and authentic way.

6. Leveraging Sponsored Content for Growth: Sponsored content can not only generate revenue but also help grow your channel. By collaborating with relevant brands, you can expand your audience, reach, and engagement. Sponsored content can also provide you with valuable networking opportunities and help you establish yourself as an authority in your niche. It's important to strike a balance between sponsored and non-sponsored content, ensuring that your channel maintains its authenticity and resonates with your audience.

7. Maintaining Brand Relationships: Building and maintaining positive relationships with sponsors is crucial for long-term success. Deliver on your commitments, follow the brand's guidelines, and provide regular updates on the performance of the sponsored content. Be professional, responsive, and reliable in your communication with sponsors. Cultivating strong brand relationships can lead to repeat sponsorships, referrals to other brands, and even potential partnerships beyond YouTube.

8. Legal Considerations: When engaging in sponsored content on YouTube, it's important to be aware of legal considerations. Familiarize yourself with the laws and regulations regarding sponsored content in your country or region, including disclosure requirements, advertising standards, and consumer protection laws. Ensure that you comply with these regulations to avoid any legal issues that could harm your channel's reputation and financial stability.

9. Tracking and Evaluating Sponsorship Performance: It's important to track the performance of your sponsored

content to assess its effectiveness and make data-driven decisions. Monitor metrics such as views, engagement, conversions, and audience feedback to understand the impact of sponsored content on your channel and your audience. Use this information to optimize your future sponsorship deals and continuously improve your content strategy.

10. Diversifying Sponsorship Opportunities: While sponsored content can be a lucrative revenue stream, it's essential to diversify your sponsorship opportunities to reduce dependence on a single brand or type of sponsorship. Explore partnerships with different brands, industries, and types of sponsored content to diversify your income streams and minimize risks. This also allows you to cater to the diverse interests and preferences of your audience, keeping your content fresh and engaging.

11. Building Your Brand as an Influencer: Sponsorships can also help you build your personal brand as an influencer. By partnering with reputable brands and creating authentic and high-quality sponsored content, you can establish yourself as an authority in your niche and attract more sponsorship opportunities in the future. Focus on building a strong and unique personal brand that resonates with your target audience and differentiates you from other YouTubers in your niche.

12. Handling Sponsorship Challenges: Sponsorships may also come with challenges, such as managing conflicting sponsorships, handling negative feedback, or dealing with demanding sponsors. It's important to have strategies in place to handle these challenges professionally and effectively. Prioritize your audience's trust and your

channel's integrity and be transparent and authentic in your communication with sponsors and your audience. Handle any challenges or conflicts with professionalism and seek guidance from experienced influencers or professionals if needed.

Sponsorships are a viable way to monetize your YouTube channel and generate revenue. With careful planning, strategic partnerships, and a commitment to providing value to your audience, sponsorships can be a valuable component of your YouTube money-making machine.

Chapter 6

Finding and Negotiating Sponsorships

As we discussed in the previous section, sponsorships are an effective way to monetize your YouTube channel and generate revenue. Brands are constantly looking for influencers and content creators to promote their products or services, and YouTube offers a platform with a massive audience that can provide immense value to brands. So, how do you find and negotiate sponsorship deals? Here's how:

1. Understanding Your Niche and Audience: Before you start searching for sponsorships, it's important to understand your niche and audience. Identify your target audience, their interests, preferences, and demographics. Understand your niche and the type of content that resonates with your audience. This understanding will help you identify potential sponsors whose products or services align with your audience's interests and preferences.

2. Researching Potential Sponsors: Once you have a clear understanding of your audience and niche, research potential sponsors who could be a good fit for your channel. Look for brands that align with your content and have a similar target audience. Check their social media profiles, websites, and online presence to assess their values, reputation, and authenticity. Look for brands that have a track record of working with influencers or content creators.

3. Reaching Out to Potential Sponsors: Once you have identified potential sponsors, it's time to reach out to them. Craft personalized and professional emails or messages

expressing your interest in partnering with them. Highlight the value you can provide to their brand and how your audience aligns with their target audience. Be concise, clear, and enthusiastic in your communication, and provide relevant information such as your channel's demographics, engagement, and reach.

4. Negotiating Sponsorship Deals: Negotiating sponsorship deals can be a crucial step in securing profitable partnerships. Be prepared to negotiate and understand your worth as an influencer. Consider factors such as your channel's reach, engagement, audience demographics, and content quality when determining your rates. Be transparent and professional in your negotiations, and be willing to compromise to reach a mutually beneficial agreement. Don't be afraid to ask questions, seek clarification, or request additional benefits such as exclusive discount codes for your audience or custom content.

5. Reviewing Sponsorship Agreements: Once you have negotiated a sponsorship deal, carefully review the sponsorship agreement before signing. Ensure that it includes all the terms and conditions that you have agreed upon, including the scope of work, deliverables, timeline, compensation, disclosure requirements, and intellectual property rights. Seek legal advice if needed, to ensure that you fully understand the terms and conditions of the agreement and protect your rights as an influencer.

6. Disclosing Sponsored Content: Disclosure is a critical aspect of sponsorship deals. As an influencer, it's important to be transparent with your audience and disclose any sponsored content in compliance with

relevant laws and regulations. Disclosures can include verbal statements, written statements in video descriptions or captions, or using tools such as YouTube's built-in disclosure features. Always prioritize the trust and integrity of your audience by clearly disclosing sponsored content and avoid misleading or deceptive practices that can harm your reputation.

7. Maintaining Authenticity and Quality: Authenticity and quality are key to building a successful and sustainable influencer brand. As you work on sponsored content, ensure that it aligns with your audience's interests and preferences and maintains the same level of authenticity and quality as your regular content. Avoid promoting products or services that you do not genuinely believe in or that are not relevant to your audience. Keep your content genuine, valuable, and engaging, and strive to provide the same level of authenticity and value to your sponsored content as your regular content.

8. Building Long-Term Relationships with Sponsors: Building long-term relationships with sponsors can be beneficial for both parties. Nurture your relationships with sponsors by delivering on your promises, providing high-quality sponsored content, and maintaining open and regular communication. Act professionally, meet deadlines, and be responsive to sponsors' feedback and requests. Building a positive working relationship with sponsors can lead to repeat collaborations, increased compensation, and opportunities for long-term partnerships.

9. Tracking and Reporting Results: It's essential to track and report the results of your sponsored content to your

sponsors. Provide detailed analytics and insights on key performance metrics such as views, engagement, click-through rates, and conversions. This data will help your sponsors assess the success of the campaign and the return on their investment. It also demonstrates your professionalism and commitment to delivering results, which can enhance your reputation as an influencer and increase your chances of securing future sponsorships.

10. Managing Expectations: Managing expectations is crucial in sponsorships. Be transparent with your sponsors about the potential outcomes of the campaign and set realistic expectations. Be clear about what you can deliver and what is not within the scope of work. Manage your sponsors' expectations in terms of the timeline, deliverables, and results. Building a relationship based on trust and honesty with your sponsors can lead to successful and mutually beneficial partnerships.

11. Being Professional and Reliable: As an influencer, it's important to maintain a professional and reliable demeanor in all your interactions with sponsors. Respond to emails or messages promptly, meet deadlines, and deliver on your promises. Be proactive in your communication and keep sponsors updated on the progress of the campaign. Demonstrate your professionalism and reliability through your actions, and it will reflect positively on your reputation as an influencer.

12. Navigating Challenges: Sponsorships may come with challenges, such as differing expectations, creative differences, or changes in campaign requirements. It's important to navigate these challenges with professionalism and adaptability. Communicate openly

and honestly with your sponsors, address any issues or concerns, and find solutions that align with the best interests of both parties. Be flexible and willing to adjust your approach or deliverables as needed, while always prioritizing the integrity of your content and the trust of your audience.

As an influencer looking to find and negotiate sponsorships on YouTube, there are several tools and resources available that can help you streamline your process and increase your chances of success. These resources can increase your chances of securing lucrative sponsorships. Here are some examples:

- Social Media Platforms: Social media platforms such as Instagram, Twitter, and LinkedIn can be valuable resources for finding and connecting with potential sponsors. You can use these platforms to search for brands or companies that align with your niche and reach out to them directly to express your interest in a collaboration.

- Brand Collaboration Platforms: There are several brand collaboration platforms that connect influencers with brands looking for sponsorships. These platforms often have a database of brands and campaigns, and you can create a profile showcasing your channel and audience demographics to attract potential sponsors. Examples of such platforms include GrapeVine, Channel Pages, and BrandSnob.

- Influencer Marketing Agencies: Influencer marketing agencies specialize in connecting influencers with brands and managing sponsorships on their behalf. These agencies often have established relationships with brands and can help you negotiate deals, manage contracts, and ensure that your interests are protected. Some popular influencer marketing agencies include GrapeVine Logic, CreatorIQ, and Obviously.

- Affiliate Marketing Networks: Many sponsors and brands use affiliate marketing to collaborate with influencers. Affiliate marketing networks such as Amazon Associates, ShareASale, and Commission Junction allow influencers to earn a commission on sales generated through their unique referral links. These networks often have a wide range of brands and products available for promotion, and you can join them and start promoting products relevant to your audience.

- Industry Events and Conferences: Industry events and conferences related to your niche can be excellent opportunities to network with potential sponsors. Many brands and agencies attend these events to scout for influencers and establish partnerships. Look for events and conferences in your industry, attend them, and take advantage of the networking opportunities they offer.

- Online Communities and Forums: There are many online communities and forums where influencers and marketers discuss sponsorships, collaborations, and other opportunities. Platforms such as Reddit, Facebook Groups, and LinkedIn Groups can be great resources for finding advice, tips, and potential sponsorship opportunities. Join relevant communities and participate in discussions to connect with like-minded individuals and learn from their experiences.

- Influencer Marketing Platforms: There are various influencer marketing platforms that act as intermediaries between influencers and brands, helping to connect them for sponsorship opportunities. These platforms typically have databases of influencers and brands, and you can create a profile to showcase your channel and attract potential sponsors. Some popular influencer marketing platforms include AspireIQ, Upfluence, and HYPR.

- Google and YouTube Search: You can also use Google and YouTube search to find potential sponsors. Use relevant keywords related to your niche and search for brands or companies that may be interested in sponsoring content creators on YouTube. Visit their websites, find their contact information, and reach out to them directly with a personalized pitch.

- Networking and Collaboration with Peers: Collaborating with other influencers in your niche can also lead to sponsorship opportunities. By working with influencers who have similar audiences, you can leverage each other's reach and influence to attract sponsors. Collaborations can also help you create valuable content and showcase your skills and professionalism to potential sponsors.

- Online Resources and Guides: There are numerous online resources and guides available that provide insights, tips, and strategies on finding and negotiating sponsorships on YouTube. Blogs, articles, e-books, and video tutorials can offer valuable guidance and advice on how to approach sponsors, negotiate deals, and build successful partnerships.

Finding and negotiating sponsorships is a valuable strategy for monetizing your YouTube that requires careful research, professional communication, and negotiation skills. By understanding your niche and audience, you can successfully navigate the world of sponsorships on YouTube.

Chapter 6

Sample Sponsor Pitch

Dear [Company's Name],

I hope this email finds you well. My name is [Your Name], and I am a content creator on YouTube with [number of subscribers] subscribers and [average view count] views per video. I am reaching out to express my interest in a potential collaboration with [Company's Name].

As an established content creator in the [your niche] niche, I have built a dedicated and engaged audience who resonates with my content. I believe that [Company's Name] could benefit from exposure to my audience through a sponsorship collaboration.

I am impressed with the values, products, and services of [Company's Name], and I believe that my audience would find them valuable and relevant. I have already used and enjoyed [mention a specific product or service from the company] in my videos, and I believe that incorporating it into my content would provide authentic and genuine promotion.

In addition to creating high-quality video content, I am also skilled in social media marketing, and I would be able to promote the collaboration on my other social media platforms, including Instagram, Twitter, and Facebook, further increasing the reach and visibility of [Company's Name].

I am open to various types of collaboration, including product reviews, sponsored videos, unboxing videos, tutorials, and more. I am also willing to discuss unique and creative ideas that align with the interests of my audience and the goals of [Company's

Name]. I am committed to delivering professional and engaging content that resonates with my audience and promotes [Company's Name] in a positive and authentic manner.

I understand the importance of disclosing sponsored content to my audience in accordance with the Federal Trade Commission (FTC) guidelines, and I am committed to full transparency and compliance with all relevant regulations.

I have successfully collaborated with other brands in the past, and my audience highly values my recommendations. I believe that a collaboration with [Company's Name] would be mutually beneficial, providing exposure to your brand and products while also generating engaging and authentic content for my audience.

I would be thrilled to discuss this collaboration opportunity further and explore how we can work together to achieve our mutual goals. Please find my media kit attached to this email, which provides more details about my channel, audience demographics, and previous collaborations.

Thank you for considering my proposal. I look forward to hearing from you and discussing this collaboration opportunity in more detail.

Sincerely,

[Your Name]

[Your YouTube Channel Name]

[Contact Information]

Here's an alternative version you can use:

Dear [Company Name],

I hope this message finds you well. My name is [Your Name] and I'm a content creator on YouTube with [Number of Subscribers] subscribers. I specialize in [Your Niche/Genre] and I create videos that are both informative and entertaining for my audience.

I'm reaching out to you today because I believe that your company and my audience would be a perfect fit. I would like to propose a sponsorship partnership where I could feature your product/service in my videos and provide my viewers with a special offer or discount.

In return, I would ask for your support in promoting my content to your followers on social media and other marketing channels. I believe that this partnership would be mutually beneficial and could help us both reach a wider audience.

Please let me know if this is something that interests you and if you would like to discuss the details further. I would be happy to provide more information about my audience demographics, engagement rates, and previous sponsored content collaborations.

Thank you for your time and consideration. I look forward to hearing from you soon.

Best regards,

[Your Name]

[Your YouTube Channel Name]

[Contact Information]

Chapter 6

Setting Rates, Deliverables, and Sponsorship Valuation Formula

One of the key aspects of successfully monetizing your YouTube channel through sponsorships is setting appropriate rates and deliverables for your partnerships. As a content creator, it's important to understand your worth and negotiate fair compensation for your valuable content and influence. Here are the most important considerations for setting rates and deliverables for YouTube sponsorships.

1. Know Your Value: Before you start setting rates and deliverables, it's crucial to understand the value you bring to the table as a YouTube content creator. Factors such as your subscriber count, engagement rate, niche, and influence within your community all play a role in determining your value to potential sponsors. Conduct research on industry standards, compare your metrics with other creators in your niche, and assess your unique strengths to establish a solid understanding of your value.

2. Consider Your Audience: Your audience is the driving force behind your YouTube channel's success, and it's important to keep their interests in mind when setting rates and deliverables for sponsorships. Consider whether the sponsored content aligns with your audience's interests and needs and ensure that the partnership feels authentic and genuine to maintain the trust you have built with your viewers.

3. Negotiate Fair Compensation: When negotiating rates with sponsors, it's crucial to be firm but fair. Consider your

time, effort, and the potential impact of the sponsored content on your channel. Avoid undervaluing yourself or settling for free products or services unless it aligns with your overall business strategy. Be prepared to negotiate and advocate for your worth while maintaining a professional and collaborative approach.

4. Define Clear Deliverables: Clearly define the deliverables you will provide to sponsors as part of the partnership. This may include creating dedicated videos, mentioning the sponsor in your videos, featuring the sponsor's logo or products, or sharing sponsored content on your social media channels. Be specific about the number of deliverables and the timeline for completion to avoid misunderstandings and ensure a smooth partnership.

5. Customize for Each Sponsor: Every sponsor is unique, and it's important to customize your rates and deliverables based on their specific needs and goals. Take the time to research the sponsor's brand, values, target audience, and marketing objectives to create a tailored proposal that highlights how your partnership can benefit their business.

6. Be Transparent: Transparency is crucial in any sponsorship partnership. Clearly disclose sponsored content to your viewers, in compliance with YouTube's guidelines and relevant laws and regulations. Be transparent about the nature of the partnership, and never compromise the trust you have built with your audience.

7. Keep Records: Maintain detailed records of your rates, deliverables, and communication with sponsors. This will help you keep track of your partnerships, ensure that both parties fulfill their commitments, and provide a reference for future negotiations.

8. Follow Up and Evaluate: After completing sponsored content, follow up with sponsors to ensure they are satisfied and gather feedback for improvement. Evaluate the impact of the partnership on your channel's performance, engagement, and revenue to refine your rates and deliverables for future sponsorships.

9. Be Professional: Lastly, always maintain a professional attitude and approach when setting rates and deliverables for YouTube sponsorships. Be responsive to sponsors' inquiries, meet deadlines, and provide high-quality content. A professional and reliable demeanor will help you build a positive reputation in the industry and attract more sponsorship opportunities.

With all this said, here is a sample valuation formula to use as a guide. Remember, this is not exact and ultimately your sponsorship is worth what a sponsor is willing to pay. This formula should be used to help you understand expectations and as a tool to help you through negotiations:

Sponsorship Valuation = (Influencer's Reach x Reach Valuation Factor) + (Engagement Rate x Engagement Rate Valuation Factor) + (Industry Factor) + (Type of Partnership Factor) + (Research Industry Rates Factor)

Where:

- Influencer's Reach: Refers to the total number of people who are exposed to the sponsored content. As a general guideline, a commonly used industry benchmark for estimating the average number of video views per followers on YouTube is 10%. This means that for every 100 followers, a video would be expected to receive around 10 views. However, it's important to note that this is a rough estimate, and the actual number can vary significantly. You should use an estimate of actual views over your most recent videos.

- Reach Valuation Factor: Represents the assigned value per reach. This can be a fixed dollar amount, or a percentage of your overall valuation based on your market research and business goals. For example, you could assign a reach valuation factor of $0.01 per reach, meaning each reach adds $0.01 to your sponsorship valuation.

- Engagement Rate: Represents the percentage of the influencer's audience who interact with their content. In this example, it's 50% of the average number of views per video, which is 250.

- Engagement Rate Valuation Factor: Represents the assigned value per engagement rate. Like the reach valuation factor, this can be a fixed dollar amount, or a percentage of your overall valuation based on your market research and business goals. As a general benchmark, the commonly used industry average for YouTube engagement rate is around 3-5%. This means that for every 100 views, a video would be expected to receive around 3-5 engagements, which can include likes, comments, shares, and subscribes. However, it's important to note that this is a rough estimate, and the actual engagement rate can vary significantly. You could assign an engagement rate valuation factor of $0.02 per engagement rate, meaning each engagement rate adds $0.02 to your sponsorship valuation.

- Industry Factor: Represents the consideration of the industry competitiveness and the influencer's niche. For example, the beauty/cosmetics industry is a popular and competitive industry, so the influencer may be able to command a higher fee. The industry factor can be a multiplier, or a fixed dollar amount added to the valuation, based on your market research and business goals.

- Type of Partnership Factor: Represents the additional work required for the specific type of partnership. For example, a sales play would require creating multiple videos and promoting the product on social media. The type of partnership factor can be a multiplier, or a fixed dollar amount added to the valuation, based on the scope of work involved.

- Research Industry Rates Factor: Represents the typical rates that other influencers in the same industry charge for sponsored content. This factor can be a benchmark or a reference point to ensure that your valuation is in line with industry standards.

It's important to note that the valuation factors, industry factor, type of partnership factor, and research industry rates factor should be determined based on your market research, business goals, and negotiation with the influencer. These factors can be adjusted to reflect the unique characteristics of the influencer, industry, and partnership, and should be agreed upon mutually between the parties involved.

Additionally, it's crucial to negotiate the fee based on the specific circumstances of the partnership and ensure that it's fair and beneficial for both parties. Setting rates and deliverables for YouTube sponsorships requires careful consideration of your value, audience, negotiation skills, customization, transparency, record-keeping, and professionalism. By taking these factors into account, you can establish fair partnerships that are mutually beneficial for you and your sponsors, and help you achieve your financial goals through your YouTube channel.

Chapter 6

Disclosing Sponsorships and Maintaining Transparency

One of the key aspects of successful YouTube monetization is maintaining transparency and disclosing sponsorships. As a content creator in the digital space, it is crucial to build trust with your audience by being upfront and transparent about any sponsored content or brand partnerships. In this section, we will explore the importance of disclosing sponsorships and maintaining transparency, along with some best practices to ensure compliance and build a loyal and engaged audience.

Why Disclosure Matters

Maintaining transparency in sponsored content is essential for building trust with your audience. Your viewers rely on your content for information, entertainment, and value. When you promote a product or service in your video, it is important to disclose any financial or material relationship you have with the brand. Disclosing sponsorships helps to establish your credibility and authenticity, and it demonstrates your commitment to transparency.

Legal Requirements

In the world of YouTube monetization, there are legal requirements that content creators need to comply with. The Federal Trade Commission (FTC) in the United States, for example, requires content creators to disclose any material connections they have with brands or products in their videos. This includes financial arrangements, free products, or any other form of compensation. It is crucial to understand and comply with these legal requirements to avoid potential legal issues and protect your reputation as a content creator.

Best Practices for Disclosure

When it comes to disclosing sponsorships and maintaining transparency, there are some best practices to keep in mind. First and foremost, disclose sponsorships clearly and conspicuously in your video or its accompanying description. Use language that is easy to understand and avoids ambiguity. For example, you can use statements like "This video is sponsored by XYZ brand" or "I received compensation from XYZ brand for this video."

Be Authentic and Genuine

Transparency goes beyond just legal requirements. It is important to be authentic and genuine in your sponsored content. Your audience can quickly detect if you are being insincere or promoting products solely for monetary gain. Build a long-term relationship with your audience by being honest, disclosing sponsorships, and only promoting products or services that align with your values and audience's interests.

Maintain Consistency

Consistency in disclosing sponsorships is key to maintaining transparency. Disclose sponsorships in all applicable videos, including those that are part of a series or a sponsored campaign. Avoid inconsistent or sporadic disclosure practices, as they can create confusion and erode trust with your audience. Make it standard practice to disclose sponsorships in a clear and consistent manner.

Educate Your Audience

In addition to disclosing sponsorships, it is also important to educate your audience about the nature of sponsorships and how they support your content. Clearly explain to your audience how sponsorships and partnerships enable you to create content and continue providing value to them. Educate your audience about the rules and regulations governing sponsored content, and how it impacts your content creation process.

Be Mindful of the Audience Experience

When creating sponsored content, always keep the audience's experience in mind. Ensure that sponsored content is seamlessly integrated into your videos and does not disrupt the viewing experience. Avoid excessive promotion or over-commercialization, as it can negatively impact your audience's perception of your content and authenticity. Strike a balance between promoting sponsored products and maintaining the integrity of your content.

Build Long-term Partnerships

Building long-term partnerships with brands can be a win-win for both parties. It allows you to create consistent sponsored content that resonates with your audience, and it provides brands with an opportunity to collaborate with a trusted influencer. When entering into brand partnerships, prioritize long-term relationships that align with your values, audience, and content. Long-term partnerships can foster transparency, trust, and authenticity, which are essential for sustained success in the world of YouTube monetization.

Stay Updated with FTC Guidelines

As a content creator, it is important to stay updated with the guidelines and regulations set forth by the Federal Trade Commission (FTC) or other relevant regulatory bodies in your country. These guidelines may evolve over time, and it is your responsibility to ensure that you follow the latest requirements. Stay informed about the latest FTC guidelines on disclosure of sponsorships, endorsements, and other related topics to ensure that you are adhering to the best practices.

Be Transparent in Other Platforms

Transparency and disclosure are not limited to YouTube alone. If you are monetizing your content on other platforms or social media channels, it is equally important to disclose sponsorships and maintain transparency across all platforms. Your audience may follow you on multiple channels, and it is crucial to maintain consistency in your disclosure practices across all platforms to ensure trust and credibility.

Consider Your Audience's Interests

When disclosing sponsorships, always consider the interests and preferences of your audience. Be mindful of the fact that your audience is there for your content, not for the sponsored products. Avoid excessive promotion or making your content feel like an extended advertisement. Prioritize the interests of your audience and ensure that your sponsored content adds value to their experience, rather than disrupting it.

Foster Open Communication with Brands

Maintaining transparency also involves fostering open communication with brands and being proactive in disclosing sponsorships. Clearly communicate your disclosure practices to brands you collaborate with and ensure that they understand your commitment to transparency. Be open to discussing any concerns or questions they may have about disclosure and work together to ensure that both parties are aligned in maintaining transparency in sponsored content.

Maintaining transparency and disclosing sponsorships are crucial aspects of monetizing your YouTube channel and building a successful career as a content creator. It is not only a legal requirement, but also an ethical obligation to your audience. By following these best practices, you can create a positive, trustworthy, and successful YouTube money-making machine that resonates with your audience and stands the test of time.

Chapter 7: YouTube Automation: The Ultimate Guide

Chapter 7

What is YouTube Automation?

YouTube automation is a powerful concept that can help content creators streamline their YouTube channel management, increase their reach, and optimize their revenue potential. It involves leveraging various tools, techniques, and strategies to automate repetitive tasks, optimize content creation and distribution, and scale channel growth. In this chapter, we will explore what YouTube automation is, why it is important, and how it can be used effectively to build a successful YouTube money-making machine.

YouTube automation refers to the use of automated tools, software, and strategies to streamline and optimize various aspects of managing a YouTube channel. This can include automating tasks such as video editing, keyword research, scheduling uploads, managing comments, and analyzing performance metrics. Automation can also involve using algorithms, data analytics, and machine learning to optimize content creation, distribution, and promotion.

YouTube automation offers several benefits for content creators looking to monetize their channels and generate passive income. Firstly, it saves time and effort by automating repetitive tasks, allowing content creators to focus on creating high-quality content and engaging with their audience. Secondly, it helps in optimizing content creation, distribution, and promotion strategies by leveraging data-driven insights and analytics. Thirdly, automation can help content creators scale their channel growth by optimizing video publishing schedules, improving search engine optimization (SEO), and increasing engagement with viewers.

YouTube automation can be categorized into various types, including content creation automation, distribution automation, engagement automation, and performance analysis automation. Content creation automation involves using tools and software for video editing, thumbnail creation, and captioning. Distribution automation involves scheduling uploads, optimizing video descriptions and tags, and leveraging social media automation for cross-promotion. Engagement automation involves managing comments, messages, and collaborations with other creators. Performance analysis automation involves using analytics tools to track video performance, audience demographics, and revenue generation.

To effectively implement YouTube automation, content creators should follow some best practices. Firstly, focus on creating high-quality, engaging, and relevant content that resonates with your target audience. Automation should not compromise the quality of your content. Secondly, stay updated with YouTube's terms of service and guidelines to ensure compliance. Thirdly, use automation tools and strategies strategically and avoid spamming or engaging in unethical practices that may harm your channel's reputation. Lastly, constantly monitor and analyze the performance of your automated strategies and adjust them as needed to optimize results.

YouTube automation can significantly impact revenue generation by optimizing content creation, distribution, and promotion strategies. For example, automated SEO techniques can help improve video rankings in search results, leading to increased organic traffic and ad revenue. Automation tools for social media promotion can help increase channel visibility, attract more viewers, and generate more sponsorship opportunities. Additionally, engagement automation can help build a loyal community of viewers who are more likely to support your channel through memberships, merchandise sales, and crowdfunding.

While YouTube automation offers numerous benefits, it also comes with some challenges and risks. Content creators should be aware of potential risks such as violating YouTube's terms of service, being flagged for spamming or engaging in unethical practices, and losing authenticity and connection with their audience. There is also a risk of relying too heavily on automation and neglecting the importance of human touch, personal engagement, and genuine content creation. Content creators should strike a balance between automation and authentic connection with their audience to build a sustainable YouTube money-making machine.

YouTube automation is an exciting opportunity for marketers new to the world of making money with YouTube, passive income, social media, and digital marketing. With the right strategies and tools in place, content creators can optimize their YouTube channel's performance, engage with their audience, and generate revenue while focusing on creating high-quality content that resonates with their viewers.

So, are you ready to unlock the power of YouTube automation and take your YouTube channel to the next level? By leveraging automation wisely and maintaining transparency, you can build a sustainable and successful YouTube money-making machine that generates revenue, engages with your audience, and brings your content creation dreams to life. Get ready to embark on an exciting journey of YouTube automation and unlock the true potential of your YouTube channel!

Chapter 7

Benefits and Drawbacks of YouTube Automation

YouTube automation can be a valuable tool for content creators looking to streamline their processes and improve their efficiency. However, it also has its drawbacks that should be taken into consideration before implementing it into your strategy.

Benefits

1. Increased productivity: One of the main benefits of YouTube automation is that it can help increase productivity. With automated processes, creators can save time on tasks such as uploading, scheduling, and promoting videos, allowing them to focus on creating more high-quality content.
2. Consistency: Another advantage of automation is that it can help ensure consistency in your content. By scheduling uploads and promoting them at regular intervals, you can maintain a steady flow of content that your audience can rely on.
3. Analytics and insights: Many automation tools come with analytics and insights features, allowing you to track the performance of your videos and identify areas for improvement.
4. Cost-effective: By automating certain tasks, you may be able to reduce the amount of time and money spent on hiring additional staff or outsourcing work.

Drawbacks

1. Lack of authenticity: One of the biggest drawbacks of YouTube automation is the potential lack of authenticity in your content. If your audience can tell that your content is automated, it may be seen as impersonal and disingenuous.
2. Limited creativity: Some automation tools may limit your creativity by forcing you to adhere to certain formats or schedules. This can be especially limiting for creators who thrive on spontaneity and flexibility.
3. Risk of errors: Although automation can save time and reduce the risk of human error, it can also introduce new risks if the tools are not properly set up or maintained. For example, automated processes may result in broken links or incorrect scheduling if not closely monitored.
4. Over-reliance on technology: Finally, over-reliance on automation tools can be dangerous if they fail or become outdated. It's important to always have a backup plan and be prepared to adapt to changes in the technology landscape.

YouTube automation can be a powerful tool for content creators, but it should be approached with caution. By weighing the benefits and drawbacks and carefully selecting the right tools for your needs, you can use automation to improve your productivity, consistency, and insights without sacrificing authenticity or creativity.

Chapter 7

Tools and Strategies for Automating YouTube Tasks

When it comes to maximizing your efficiency and productivity as a content creator on YouTube, automation can be a game-changer. By automating certain tasks, you can save time, streamline your workflow, and focus on creating high-quality content that resonates with your audience. Are you ready to take your YouTube game to the next level? Let's dive in and discover the world of YouTube automation together!

1. Content scheduling tools: One of the key tasks that can be automated on YouTube is content scheduling. There are several tools available, such as TubeBuddy, VidIQ, and Hootsuite, that allow you to schedule your video uploads in advance. You can set specific dates and times for your videos to go live, ensuring a consistent publishing schedule without having to manually upload each video.

2. Social media automation tools: Social media is an important aspect of promoting your YouTube content, and it can also be automated. Tools like Buffer, Later, and Sprout Social allow you to schedule and automate your social media posts across multiple platforms, such as Instagram, Twitter, and Facebook, to promote your YouTube videos and engage with your audience.

3. Email marketing automation tools: Email marketing can be a powerful tool for promoting your YouTube content and building a loyal audience. With email marketing automation tools like Mailchimp, ConvertKit, and AWeber, you can automate the process of sending out newsletters, updates, and announcements to your

subscribers, keeping them informed about your latest videos and encouraging them to engage with your content.

4. Comment moderation tools: Managing comments on your YouTube videos can be time-consuming, but with comment moderation tools like YouTube Studio, Disqus, and Social Blade, you can automate the process of filtering and moderating comments. These tools allow you to set up filters, block certain keywords or users, and automatically hide or delete inappropriate comments, saving you time and ensuring a positive comment section on your videos.

5. Analytics and reporting tools: Monitoring the performance of your YouTube videos is crucial for optimizing your content and strategy. With analytics and reporting tools like YouTube Analytics, Google Analytics, and Social Blade, you can automate the process of tracking key metrics such as views, engagement, and audience demographics, allowing you to make data-driven decisions and improve your content performance.

6. Video editing software: Editing your videos can be time-consuming, but with video editing software like Adobe Premiere Pro, Final Cut Pro, and iMovie, you can automate certain tasks to speed up the process. Features such as batch editing, templates, and presets allow you to apply consistent effects, transitions, and edits across multiple videos, saving you time and maintaining a cohesive visual style.

7. Collaborations and partnerships: Collaborating with other content creators can be a powerful way to grow your audience and increase your reach on YouTube. By using collaboration and partnership management tools like GrapeVine, Channel Pages, and BrandSnob, you can

automate the process of finding, connecting, and negotiating collaborations with other creators, saving you time and effort in the outreach process.

8. Affiliate marketing tools: If you monetize your YouTube channel through affiliate marketing, there are tools available that can help you automate the process. Tools like Amazon Associates, ShareASale, and Commission Junction allow you to automate the tracking, reporting, and payment of affiliate commissions, making it easier to manage your affiliate partnerships and maximize your earnings.

In addition to these tools, there are several strategies you can implement to effectively automate your YouTube tasks:

1. Develop a content calendar: Creating a content calendar in advance can help you plan and schedule your videos, social media posts, and other promotional activities. This allows you to batch-process tasks, such as video uploads, social media posts, and email newsletters, and automate them using the appropriate tools.

2. Create templates and presets: Developing templates and presets for your video editing software, social media posts, and email newsletters can save you time and effort. You can create reusable templates with pre-designed graphics, fonts, and formatting that can be easily applied to new videos, posts, and newsletters, ensuring consistent branding and style across your content.

3. Set up automations in your email marketing software: Most email marketing platforms offer automation features that allow you to create automated email sequences based on triggers, such as new subscribers, video uploads, or

specific actions taken by your audience. You can set up automated welcome emails, follow-up emails, and promotional emails to engage with your audience without having to manually send each email.

4. Use social media scheduling tools: As mentioned earlier, social media scheduling tools like Buffer, Later, and Sprout Social allow you to automate your social media posts across multiple platforms. You can create a content calendar, schedule your posts in advance, and even automate the process of recycling and repurposing your old content, saving you time and effort in managing your social media presence.

5. Utilize batch processing: Batch processing involves grouping similar tasks together and completing them all at once, rather than doing them individually. For example, you can batch record several videos in one sitting, batch edit them, and then batch upload them to YouTube using scheduling tools. This can save you time and increase your efficiency, allowing you to focus on other important aspects of your content creation process.

6. Outsource repetitive tasks: If you have the budget, consider outsourcing repetitive tasks, such as video editing, transcribing, or social media scheduling, to virtual assistants or freelancers. This can free up your time to focus on creating high-quality content while leaving the repetitive tasks to others who can handle them efficiently.

7. Regularly review and optimize your automated processes: It's important to regularly review and optimize your automated processes to ensure they are still effective and aligned with your goals. Monitor the performance of your automated tasks, review the analytics and data, and adjust

as needed to continuously improve your automation strategies.

While automation can offer numerous benefits in terms of timesaving, efficiency, and productivity, it's also important to consider the drawbacks. Here are some potential drawbacks of YouTube automation:

1. Loss of authenticity: Automation can sometimes lead to a loss of authenticity in your content, as it may come across as too automated or robotic. It's important to strike a balance between automation and personalization to maintain an authentic connection with your audience.

2. Risk of errors: Automated processes are not always foolproof, and there is a risk of errors or glitches occurring. For example, scheduled posts may not go live as planned, or automated emails may end up in spam folders. It's crucial to double-check and monitor your automated processes to ensure they are functioning correctly.

3. Dependence on third-party tools: Most automation strategies rely on third-party tools or software, which may have limitations, require ongoing subscriptions or updates, or even cease to exist. It's essential to be aware of the risks and have contingency plans in place in case any of your automation tools become unavailable.

4. Reduced personal touch: Automation can sometimes result in a reduced personal touch in your interactions with your audience. Automated responses or generic templates may not resonate with your audience as much as personalized interactions. It's important to balance

automation with genuine human engagement to maintain a strong connection with your audience.

Automation can be a valuable tool for optimizing your YouTube content creation process and maximizing your efficiency as a content creator. With the right tools and strategies, you can turn your YouTube channel into a well-oiled money-making machine, freeing up your time and resources to focus on creating content that resonates with your audience and drives revenue.

Chapter 8: Thinking Outside of the Box

Chapter 8

Out-of-the-Box Ways to Monetize YouTube

Throughout this book, we have discussed the traditional ways to make money on YouTube, such as through ad revenue, sponsored content, and affiliate marketing. However, there are many unique and creative ways to monetize your YouTube channel that go beyond the conventional methods. Here is a comprehensive list of out-of-the-box ways to make money on YouTube:

1. Merchandise sales: If you have a loyal fan base, consider creating and selling merchandise related to your YouTube channel, such as t-shirts, mugs, or posters. You can use platforms like Teespring or Shopify to design and sell your merchandise directly to your audience.

2. Crowdfunding: Platforms like Patreon or Kickstarter allow you to raise funds from your audience to support your content creation. You can offer exclusive perks, behind-the-scenes access, or other incentives to your supporters in exchange for their financial support.

3. Online courses: If you have expertise in a particular field, consider creating and selling online courses related to your niche. You can use platforms like Udemy or Teachable to create and sell courses on topics that are relevant to your audience.

4. Fan engagement services: Offer personalized services to your fans, such as shoutouts, personalized videos, or one-on-one consultations, for a fee. This can be a unique way to connect with your audience and offer them a personalized experience.

5. Crowdsourced content: Involve your audience in creating content for your channel by asking them for ideas, suggestions, or submissions. You can then compile and feature the best contributions in your videos and monetize the content through ads or sponsorships.

6. Licensing your content: If you create unique and original content, you can consider licensing it to other platforms, such as TV networks, streaming services, or brands. This can provide an additional stream of revenue for your content.

7. Product reviews: Review products or services related to your niche and earn commission through affiliate marketing. You can provide honest and valuable reviews and include affiliate links in your video descriptions to earn a commission when your viewers make a purchase through your links.

8. Public speaking engagements: If you have a compelling story or expertise in your niche, you can leverage your YouTube channel to get invitations for public speaking engagements at conferences, events, or workshops. This can be a lucrative opportunity to share your knowledge and earn speaking fees.

9. Sponsorship deals: Beyond sponsored content, you can explore unique sponsorship opportunities, such as sponsored events, branded content series, or sponsored trips. Be creative in identifying potential sponsors and negotiating mutually beneficial partnerships.

10. Donations and tips: If your content resonates with your audience, you can ask for donations or tips from your viewers. Platforms like Patreon, Ko-fi, or Buy Me a

Coffee allow you to accept donations or tips from your audience as a way to support your content.

11. Voice-over work: If you have a distinctive voice or narration skills, you can offer voice-over services to other content creators, video producers, or companies. You can charge a fee for your services and provide voice-over work for their videos or commercials.

12. Brand collaborations: Collaborate with other YouTubers, influencers, or brands on unique projects or campaigns. This can help you expand your reach, gain new viewers, and earn revenue through collaborative efforts.

There are countless out-of-the-box ways to make money on YouTube beyond the conventional methods. By being creative you can explore unique monetization opportunities that align with your content and niche. Always ensure that any monetization methods you choose are compliant with YouTube's policies and guidelines and strive to provide value to your audience while building a sustainable and profitable YouTube channel.

Chapter 8

Out-of-the-Box Niches for your YouTube Channel

One of the keys to building a successful YouTube money making machine is to find a niche that sets you apart from the competition. While there are plenty of popular niches on YouTube, thinking outside the box and exploring unique niches can be a game-changer. In this section, we will delve into the world of out-of-the-box niches and how you can leverage them to create engaging content, grow your audience, and make money on YouTube.

1. Unconventional Hobbies: Hobbies are a great source of content for YouTube. Consider unique hobbies that are not commonly covered, such as rock climbing, origami, or mushroom foraging. By creating content around unconventional hobbies, you can tap into a passionate and dedicated audience who are eager to learn and engage with like-minded individuals.

2. Alternative Lifestyles: Alternative lifestyles are gaining popularity, and YouTube provides a platform to showcase and document these lifestyles. From van life to minimalism, tiny homes to eco-friendly living, there are numerous alternative lifestyles that can make for captivating content. Share your experiences, tips, and challenges to attract an audience interested in these unconventional ways of living.

3. Cultural Exploration: Cultural exploration can be a fascinating niche to explore on YouTube. Dive into lesser-known cultures, traditions, and practices from around the world. Share your insights, experiences, and stories about

different cultures, their history, and their unique way of life. This can help you create educational and immersive content that appeals to curious viewers.

4. Niche Art Forms: Art comes in many forms, and showcasing niche art forms on YouTube can be intriguing. Whether it's calligraphy, pottery, or glassblowing, creating content that highlights these lesser-known art forms can capture the attention of art enthusiasts and provide a fresh perspective on the world of art.

5. Rare Collectibles: Collectibles are a niche that has a dedicated following. If you have a passion for collecting rare items such as vintage toys, stamps, or coins, share your collection, knowledge, and experiences on YouTube. This can attract fellow collectors and enthusiasts who are interested in rare and unique collectibles.

6. Sustainable Living: As awareness about sustainability grows, creating content around sustainable living can be a unique niche on YouTube. Share tips on reducing waste, living a zero-waste lifestyle, or sustainable fashion and beauty. This can resonate with viewers who are looking for ways to live an eco-friendlier lifestyle and make a positive impact on the planet.

7. DIY and Upcycling: DIY and upcycling are gaining popularity as people seek creative ways to repurpose and recycle items. Create content that showcases DIY projects, upcycling ideas, and crafts using everyday items. This can attract viewers who are interested in DIY projects and eco-friendly solutions for their everyday lives.

8. Extreme Sports: Extreme sports are always thrilling and captivating to watch. If you're into activities such as parkour, skateboarding, or snowboarding, create content

that showcases your skills, challenges, and adventures. This can attract adrenaline junkies and sports enthusiasts who are interested in extreme sports and are looking for unique perspectives and experiences.

9. Science and Technology: Science and technology are constantly evolving, and there are numerous unique niches to explore in this field. From futuristic gadgets and inventions to cutting-edge research and breakthroughs, creating content that showcases the latest developments in science and technology can attract tech-savvy viewers who are interested in staying updated with the latest trends and innovations.

10. Urban exploration: Showcasing abandoned buildings, forgotten places, and hidden urban gems can be intriguing for viewers who are fascinated by the mysteries and stories behind these forgotten spaces.

11. Ghost hunting: If you have an interest in the paranormal, you can create content around ghost hunting, investigating haunted locations, and sharing your eerie experiences with your audience.

12. ASMR: Autonomous Sensory Meridian Response (ASMR) is a phenomenon where certain sounds or visuals trigger pleasurable sensations for viewers. Creating ASMR content such as whispering, tapping, or soothing sounds can be a niche that has a dedicated following.

13. Astrology and tarot: If you have knowledge and expertise in astrology or tarot readings, you can create content around these topics, providing insights, tutorials, and readings for your viewers who are interested in divination and spirituality.

14. Toy unboxing and reviews: Unboxing and reviewing toys can be a niche that appeals to younger audiences who are passionate about collectible toys, action figures, dolls, and other playthings.

15. Historical reenactments: If you have a passion for history, you can create content by reenacting historical events, wearing period costumes, and providing insights into different eras and civilizations.

Exploring out-of-the-box niches can be a game-changer in building a successful YouTube money making machine. By thinking outside the box and delving into unique niches, you can create engaging content that stands out in a crowded YouTube landscape. The key is to be authentic, passionate, and provide valuable insights, experiences, and stories that captivate viewers' attention. So, go ahead and explore the uncharted territories of YouTube niches, and let your imagination run wild as you embark on your journey to become a YouTube money making machine.

Chapter 9: Growing Your Channel and Maximizing Revenue

Chapter 9

Growing Your Channel and Increasing Reach

Now that you've set up your channel, found your niche, optimized for monetization, and created compelling content, it's time to focus on growing your channel and increasing your reach. Here are some practical tips and strategies to help you expand your YouTube presence and attract more viewers.

1. Understand your target audience: Understanding your target audience is crucial for creating content that resonates with them. Research your audience's demographics, interests, preferences, and viewing habits. This will help you tailor your content to their needs and preferences and create videos that are engaging and relevant to them.

2. Optimize your video titles, descriptions, and tags: YouTube is a search-based platform, and optimizing your video titles, descriptions, and tags can significantly improve your video's discoverability. Use relevant keywords that your target audience is likely to search for and make sure to include them in your video titles, descriptions, and tags to increase your video's visibility in search results.

3. Create compelling thumbnails: Thumbnails are like mini movie posters that represent your video in search results and suggested videos. Create visually appealing and relevant thumbnails that entice viewers to click on your videos. Use bold and clear text, high-quality images, and vibrant colors to make your thumbnails stand out and attract viewers' attention.

4. Collaborate with other YouTubers: Collaborating with other YouTubers in your niche can help you tap into their audience and expand your reach. Look for opportunities to collaborate with creators who have similar content and audience as yours. Collaborative videos can bring fresh perspectives, new viewers, and increased engagement to your channel.

5. Promote your videos on other social media platforms: Don't limit your promotional efforts to YouTube alone. Leverage other social media platforms, such as Instagram, Twitter, Facebook, and TikTok, to promote your videos, engage with your audience, and drive traffic to your YouTube channel. Cross-promoting your videos on multiple platforms can help you reach a wider audience and increase your channel's visibility.

6. Engage with your audience: Building a loyal and engaged audience is crucial for growing your YouTube channel. Respond to comments on your videos, engage with your viewers on social media, and encourage them to participate in discussions and share their feedback. This will help you build a community around your channel and foster a sense of connection with your audience.

7. Consistency is key: Consistency is essential in growing your YouTube channel. Regularly upload high-quality content and stick to a consistent posting schedule. This will help you build momentum, keep your audience engaged, and establish your channel as a reliable source of content in your niche.

8. Analyze and optimize your performance: YouTube provides a wealth of analytics and insights about your channel's performance. Monitor your video's performance,

analyze the data, and identify trends and patterns. Use this information to optimize your content, understand what resonates with your audience, and make data-driven decisions to grow your channel.

9. Use end screens and annotations: End screens and annotations are powerful tools to promote your other videos, playlists, or even external websites at the end of your videos. Use them strategically to encourage viewers to watch more of your content, subscribe to your channel, and explore your other videos.

10. Experiment with different content formats: Don't be afraid to experiment with different content formats to keep your channel fresh and engaging. Try different types of videos, such as tutorials, vlogs, Q&A sessions, behind-the-scenes, and more. Keep an eye on the performance of different formats and iterate on what works best for your audience.

11. Collaborate with brands and monetize your channel: Once you've built a significant following, you can explore opportunities for brand partnerships, sponsored content, product reviews, and other ways to monetize your channel. Collaborating with brands can not only generate revenue but also provide unique and valuable content for your audience. Be sure to comply with YouTube's guidelines and disclose any sponsored content to maintain transparency and trust with your audience.

12. Stay updated with YouTube's policies and best practices: YouTube's policies and best practices are constantly evolving, and it's important to stay updated with them to ensure compliance and optimize your channel's performance. Keep yourself informed about YouTube's guidelines, copyright policies, community guidelines, and

monetization rules to avoid any violations that could impact your channel's growth.

Success on YouTube takes time and effort, so be patient, stay consistent, and keep experimenting with new ideas and strategies. With dedication and perseverance, your YouTube channel can become a thriving money-making machine that generates passive income and opens exciting opportunities in the world of digital marketing and social media.

Chapter 9

Building a Loyal Audience

Building a loyal audience is a key aspect of successful YouTube channel growth. When you have a dedicated group of viewers who regularly engage with your content, share it with others, and eagerly await your next upload, you create a strong foundation for monetizing your channel and making money on YouTube. Here are some highly effective strategies for building a loyal audience on YouTube.

1. Know your target audience: Understanding your target audience is essential for creating content that resonates with them. Research your audience's interests, preferences, and demographics, and tailor your content accordingly. Use YouTube analytics to gain insights into your audience's behavior, demographics, and interests, and use this information to inform your content creation strategy.

2. Create compelling content: Content is king on YouTube, and creating high-quality, engaging, and valuable content is crucial for building a loyal audience. Focus on producing videos that are informative, entertaining, and relevant to your target audience's interests. Use storytelling, humor, visuals, and other creative elements to make your content memorable and shareable.

3. Be consistent: Consistency is key to building a loyal audience on YouTube. Regularly upload new videos on a consistent schedule to keep your audience engaged and interested. Aim for a posting frequency that is manageable for you and aligns with your audience's expectations.

4. Engage with your audience: Building a loyal audience requires engaging with your viewers and building a community around your channel. Respond to comments, ask for feedback, and encourage your viewers to share their thoughts and opinions. This helps foster a sense of connection and loyalty among your audience.

5. Use social media to promote your content: Leverage the power of social media to promote your YouTube content and build a loyal audience. Share your videos on other social media platforms where your target audience is active, and use engaging captions, hashtags, and visuals to encourage clicks and shares.

6. Collaborate with other YouTubers: Collaborating with other YouTubers can be a powerful strategy for building a loyal audience. Look for creators in your niche or with a similar target audience and collaborate on videos, cross-promote each other's channels, and tap into each other's audiences to expand your reach.

7. Offer unique and exclusive content: Providing exclusive content or perks to your loyal audience can be a great way to build loyalty. Consider offering behind-the-scenes footage, special discounts, or access to exclusive events to reward your most engaged viewers and keep them coming back for more.

8. Use calls to action (CTAs): Encourage your viewers to act by including clear and compelling calls to action (CTAs) in your videos. Ask them to subscribe, like, share, comment, or follow you on social media. CTAs help drive engagement, build loyalty, and increase audience interaction.

9. Optimize your channel page: Your channel page is your online hub on YouTube and optimizing it can help you build a loyal audience. Make sure your channel banner, profile picture, and channel description clearly communicate your content and brand identity. Organize your videos into playlists, add relevant tags, and use keywords to optimize your channel for search.

10. Be authentic and genuine: Authenticity and genuineness are highly valued by YouTube viewers. Be yourself, share your story, and connect with your audience on a personal level. Show your passion, expertise, and unique perspective to build a genuine connection with your viewers and foster loyalty.

11. Listen to feedback and adapt: Pay attention to feedback from your audience and adapt your content accordingly. Use comments, messages, and social media interactions as an opportunity to understand your audience's needs, preferences, and concerns. Incorporate their feedback into your content creation strategy to build a loyal audience that feels heard and valued.

12. Be patient and persistent: Building a loyal audience takes time and effort, so be patient and persistent. Rome wasn't built in a day, and neither will your YouTube channel. Keep creating high-quality content, engaging with your audience, and promoting your channel consistently. It's important to stay committed to your content and audience, even if you don't see instant results. Building a loyal audience is a long-term goal, and it requires consistent effort and dedication.

Remember, building a loyal audience takes time and effort, but with the right strategies and a genuine commitment to your audience, you can create a thriving YouTube channel that generates passive income and brings you success in the world of digital marketing. Keep implementing these strategies and watch your YouTube channel become a money-making machine!

Chapter 9

Maximize your Earnings Potential

As a content creator on YouTube, maximizing your earnings potential is crucial to turning your channel into a profitable venture. In this section, we will explore strategies and tips to help you optimize your earnings on YouTube and make the most out of your content creation efforts.

1. Create High-Quality Content: The foundation of any successful YouTube channel is high-quality content. Focus on creating videos that are engaging, informative, and valuable to your target audience. Invest in good equipment, such as a quality camera and microphone, to ensure professional-looking videos with good audio quality. Consider the visual and audio aspects of your videos, as well as the content itself, to deliver a compelling viewing experience that keeps your audience coming back for more.

2. Optimize Video Titles, Descriptions, and Tags: Optimizing your video titles, descriptions, and tags is essential for search engine optimization (SEO) on YouTube. Use relevant keywords in your video titles, descriptions, and tags to help your videos rank higher in search results. Consider what terms your target audience might be searching for and incorporate them strategically in your video metadata to increase visibility and attract more viewers.

3. Monetize Your Videos: Take advantage of YouTube's monetization features to earn money from your videos. Join the YouTube Partner Program (YPP) and enable ads

on your videos to earn ad revenue. You can also explore other monetization options, such as merchandise sales, channel memberships, or Super Chat and Super Stickers, which allow your viewers to support you financially during live streams.

4. Diversify Your Revenue Streams: As discussed throughout this book, diversifying your revenue streams is essential for maximizing your earnings potential. Don't rely solely on YouTube ad revenue, but explore other opportunities such as brand partnerships, affiliate marketing, merchandise sales, or crowdfunding to diversify your income sources and increase your earnings.

5. Engage with Your Audience: Building a loyal and engaged audience is key to maximizing your earnings potential on YouTube. Respond to comments on your videos, engage with your audience on social media, and create a community around your channel. Encourage your viewers to like, comment, and share your videos, and ask for feedback to improve your content. By building a strong relationship with your audience, you can increase their loyalty and support, leading to higher earnings potential.

6. Collaborate with Other Creators: Collaborating with other creators can expand your reach and increase your earnings potential. Look for creators in your niche or related niches and collaborate on videos, campaigns, or events. Collaborations can introduce your channel to new audiences and help you gain more visibility and subscribers, ultimately leading to higher earnings potential.

7. Use Affiliate Marketing: Affiliate marketing is a powerful way to monetize your YouTube channel and maximize

your earnings. Promote products or services that are relevant to your audience in your videos and include affiliate links in your descriptions or within the videos themselves. Earn a commission for each sale or conversion made through your affiliate links and choose products or services that align with your channel's niche and audience for better results.

8. Utilize Social Media for Promotion: Social media can be a valuable tool for promoting your YouTube channel and increasing your earnings potential. Create a strong presence on social media platforms such as Instagram, Twitter, Facebook, or TikTok, and use them to promote your videos, engage with your audience, and drive traffic to your YouTube channel. Utilize social media advertising, hashtags, and collaborations with influencers to reach a wider audience and attract more viewers to your channel.

9. Optimize Your Channel's Branding: A cohesive and professional branding can help you stand out from the competition and increase your earnings potential. Optimize your channel's branding, including your channel banner, profile picture, and thumbnails, to create a visually appealing and consistent look for your channel. Use eye-catching thumbnails with clear titles and images that represent the content of your videos. Your branding should reflect your channel's niche and target audience and convey a professional image that attracts viewers and potential brand partnerships.

10. Offer Value-Added Services: Consider offering value-added services to your audience to generate additional revenue. This could include creating an online course,

offering consulting or coaching services, or selling digital products such as eBooks or templates. Identify the needs of your audience and offer services or products that provide value and solve their problems, while also generating income for you.

11. Utilize Patreon or Crowdfunding Platforms: Patreon and other crowdfunding platforms can be a great way to generate additional income from your YouTube channel. Set up a Patreon account and offer exclusive content or perks to your patrons in exchange for their support. You can also use crowdfunding platforms to raise funds for special projects, merchandise production, or other business expenses.

12. Leverage Analytics and Insights: Utilize the analytics and insights provided by YouTube to gain a deeper understanding of your audience and video performance. Monitor your video metrics, such as views, watch time, engagement, and demographics, to identify trends and patterns. Use this data to optimize your content strategy, understand what resonates with your audience, and make informed decisions to maximize your earnings potential.

Maximizing your earnings potential on YouTube requires a strategic approach that goes beyond just ad revenue. It can provide you with a sustainable source of income, allowing you to monetize your passion and creativity. It also offers opportunities for diversifying revenue streams, creating financial stability, and growing your online business, providing you with greater financial freedom and flexibility.

Chapter 10: Your Journey Begins Today

Chapter 10

Key Takeaways

Congratulations! You have now reached the final chapter of this book, "Making Money on YouTube Without Making Videos," and have gained valuable insights into how to make money on YouTube, create passive income, and leverage social media and digital marketing to grow your online business. Here are some key takeaways to keep in mind as you embark on your YouTube money-making journey:

1. Find your niche: Identifying a unique and profitable niche for your YouTube channel is crucial. It's important to choose a niche that aligns with your passion, expertise, and target audience.

2. Create high-quality content: Producing engaging and high-quality content should be your top priority. Invest in good equipment, optimize your videos for search engines, and focus on delivering value to your viewers.

3. Build a loyal audience: Building a loyal audience is key to your success on YouTube. Engage with your viewers, respond to comments, and build a community around your content. This will help you establish a dedicated fan base that will support your channel.

4. Monetize your channel: There are various ways to monetize your YouTube channel, such as through ads, sponsored content, merchandise, and crowdfunding. Explore different revenue streams and diversify your income to maximize your earnings potential.

5. Automate and optimize: Utilize tools and strategies to automate repetitive tasks and optimize your channel for

growth. This includes scheduling, analytics, SEO, and leveraging social media to promote your content.

6. Stay consistent and persistent: Success on YouTube takes time and effort. Stay consistent with your content creation schedule, be persistent in your marketing efforts, and keep learning and adapting to the ever-evolving YouTube landscape.

7. Be authentic and genuine: Authenticity and genuineness are valued by viewers. Be yourself, share your story, and connect with your audience on a personal level. This will help you build trust and loyalty among your viewers.

8. Continuously improve: Keep learning, improving, and evolving as a content creator. Stay updated with YouTube trends, algorithms, and best practices. Experiment with new content ideas, formats, and strategies to stay ahead of the competition.

9. Stay patient and resilient: Building a successful YouTube channel takes time and perseverance. It's important to stay patient, stay positive, and stay resilient in the face of challenges and setbacks. Remember, success is a journey, not an overnight destination.

10. Enjoy the process: Finally, enjoy the process of creating content, engaging with your audience, and growing your YouTube channel. Embrace the excitement, creativity, and opportunities that YouTube offers and have fun along the way.

Making money on YouTube can be a fulfilling and lucrative endeavor. By following the tips and strategies outlined in this book, you can create a thriving YouTube channel, generate passive income, and achieve your financial goals. Remember, it's not just about making money, but also about creating meaningful content, building a loyal audience, and enjoying the journey of being a successful YouTuber.

Chapter 10

Final Thoughts

Starting a YouTube channel and monetizing it can be a challenging but rewarding endeavor. It's normal to feel a mix of excitement and apprehension, especially if you are new to this world. However, remember that every successful YouTuber started from scratch at some point. You have the potential to achieve your financial and creative goals through YouTube, and the possibilities are endless.

One of the first steps in getting started is to believe in yourself and your abilities. You have unique skills, knowledge, and perspectives that you can share with the world through your YouTube channel. Embrace your strengths and use them to create content that resonates with your target audience. Remember, you don't need to be a professional videographer or have a large budget to start. Your passion, creativity, and authenticity can outweigh technical limitations.

It's also important to set realistic expectations for yourself. Building a successful YouTube channel takes time, effort, and dedication. It's not an overnight success story, but a journey that requires consistent and persistent action. Don't be discouraged by slow growth or initial challenges. Keep learning, improving, and adapting as you progress. Success may not come right away, but with patience and perseverance, you can achieve your goals.

Surrounding yourself with a supportive community can also greatly contribute to your motivation and success. Connect with other YouTubers, join online forums or groups, and seek mentorship from experienced creators. Surrounding yourself with like-minded individuals who share your passion for YouTube and monetization can provide you with encouragement, inspiration, and valuable insights.

As you embark on your YouTube money-making journey, remember to enjoy the process. YouTube is a platform for creativity, self-expression, and community building. Have fun experimenting with different content ideas, formats, and styles. Embrace the joy of creating content that resonates with your viewers and be open to feedback and constructive criticism.

It's also important to keep a positive mindset and stay motivated even in the face of challenges. There may be times when you encounter setbacks, face rejection, or feel overwhelmed. During these times, it's crucial to stay resilient, persevere, and keep pushing forward. Remember your "why" – the reasons why you wanted to start your YouTube channel in the first place – and let it fuel your motivation to keep going.

Don't be afraid to dream big and set ambitious goals for yourself. With hard work, dedication, and strategic planning, you can achieve extraordinary results. Visualize your success, set specific and measurable goals, and create a roadmap to guide your progress. Celebrate your milestones along the way and use them as motivation to keep pushing yourself.

Lastly, remember that you are in charge of creating your own success story on YouTube. The world of YouTube monetization and passive income is constantly evolving, and there are always new opportunities to explore. Trust in your abilities, stay committed to your goals, and be open to learning and adapting. You have the potential to create a thriving YouTube channel, generate passive income, and live life on your own terms. You are now equipped with the knowledge, strategies, and motivation to start your own YouTube monetization journey. Embrace the excitement, creativity, and possibilities that YouTube offers, and take action to turn your dreams into reality. Best of luck on your YouTube money-making adventure!

MAKING MONEY ON YOUTUBE WITHOUT MAKING VIDEOS

A Message from The Author

Dear Reader,

Thank you for taking the time to read *Making Money on YouTube Without Making Videos*. I hope you found it informative and helpful in your own journey to exploring & better understanding the world of making money on YouTube, with or without videos.

As an author, the feedback I receive from readers like you is invaluable in helping me to continue to improve my writing and create content that is relevant and useful. That's why I would like to ask you to take a few minutes to leave a rating and review on Amazon.

Not only does your review help me to know what I'm doing right and where I can improve, but it also helps other readers who are considering purchasing the book to make an informed decision. Your words have the power to influence others and to help them succeed in their own journey.

I would greatly appreciate your honest feedback, whether it's positive or negative. Your insights will not only help me to become a better writer, but they will also help other readers to benefit from the knowledge and experience that I've shared in this book.

Thank you again for your support and for taking the time to leave a review. It means the world to me.

Best regards,

Alex

www.ingramcontent.com/pod-product-compliance
Lightning Source LLC
Chambersburg PA
CBHW072149230526
45467CB00041B/1133